Comedy Minus Time: Misadventures in Romance, Marginal Comments, and Other Non-Sequiturs

What do you get when an aging millennial authors a book which draws more inspiration from music, film, and television than from other novels? A contemporary, self-aware work that innovatively plays with time and perspectives, *Comedy Minus Time* defies categorization, positioned somewhere between memoir, therapy notes, and satirical examination of masculinity in pop culture. Imagine Fleetwood Mac's *Rumours* meets Marvel's *Deadpool* meets a term paper based on the assigned reading of Nick Hornby's *High Fidelity* for your graduate level Gender Studies class. When human civilization is wiped out, alien cultures may well refer to this text as the primary source for understanding the melancholic millennial male.

Comedy Minus Time

Misadventures in Romance,
Marginal Comments,
and other Non-Sequiturs

Adam Martin

ARCHWAY
PUBLISHING

Archway Publishing books may be ordered through booksellers or by contacting:

Archway Publishing
1663 Liberty Drive
Bloomington, IN 47403
www.archwaypublishing.com
844-669-3957

Because of the dynamic nature of the Internet, any web addresses or links contained in this book may have changed since publication and may no longer be valid. The views expressed in this work are solely those of the author and do not necessarily reflect the views of the publisher, and the publisher hereby disclaims any responsibility for them.

Any people depicted in stock imagery provided by Getty Images are models, and such images are being used for illustrative purposes only.
Certain stock imagery © Getty Images.

Interior Image Credit: Isabella Carapella

ISBN: 978-1-6657-3555-1 (sc)
ISBN: 978-1-6657-3554-4 (e)

Library of Congress Control Number: 2022923493

Print information available on the last page.

Archway Publishing rev. date: 02/10/2023

Writing this book would not have been possible were it not for the support of Agnes, Agatha, Jermaine, and Jack, whose friendship, above all else, remains factual.

CONTENTS

INTRODUCTION

As any self-respecting former almost-scientist would do, I had to sit down and look at some data. It had been roughly nine years since I had dated anyone for longer than three months, which was, in itself, an empirical revelation and statistical near impossibility. After my most recent breakup, I felt compelled to really engage with the source material of my romantic misfortunes in a way I never had before, in the hope of discovering something I had never really known before. What follows is a roughly chronological, thorough, but not comprehensive account of my past relationships.

If this ends up being any good, a great deal of credit is owed to *BoJack Horseman* creator Raphael Bob-Waksberg, writer Joanna Calo, and illustrator/production designer Lisa Hanawalt. The brutal honesty embodied by all characters, particularly Diane Nguyen (especially in the episode "Good Damage") struck me like a lightning bolt and empowered me to write about my own experience. Also, special thanks to Dan Harmon for creating the immersive and surreally real world of *Community* and for breathing air into the incomparably meta and loveable Abed Nadir. It should go without saying that fellow *Community* actor/Renaissance man Donald Glover is an inspiration to everyone who has watched, heard, or read any of his work and appreciates his commitment to authenticity to his self and visions. Much the same can be said of Alanis Morrissette's *Jagged Little Pill*, among countless other popular culture touchstones that have been built upon personal truths more than the explicit goal to become popular.

But if this ends up being a sophomoric, whiny piece of prose dripping with unchecked privilege and fails to resonate with those who read it, none of the aforementioned artists and works of art played much of a role in the following musings and writings. It will have been a self-contained, underwhelming brooding apparatus—or SCUBA, for short.

PROLOGUE

CRACKED REAR VIEW[i]

You had already committed to emotional processing through writing a week or two prior, and the similarities between your experience and *Forgetting Sarah Marshall*[1] were uncanny.[2] Flying to Hawaii by yourself on the weekend of Saint Valentine's Day on the heels of a rough breakup was not an homage by design but one you grew to thoroughly appreciate. Fate, destiny, and providence were empty concepts to you, but what a hilarious coincidence this was becoming. You embraced the ridiculousness.

At one point, you had even used the name of the *Sarah Marshall* protagonist, Peter Bretter, as your moniker on a dating

1. It's that tired Hollywood trope of boy-meets-girl after she's been cheating on him for a year with an international superstar musician, and they all mistakenly meet up in Oahu, even though no one is quite over the breakup yet. Oh, and there is a musical about Dracula performed by Jim Henson puppeteers.

website. Although this trip started out as a desperate last-minute attempt to make the most of a long weekend, the line between coincidence and perceived destiny obscured constantly.[3]

Once aboard the plane for a few hours, you were handed a seemingly standard declarations form. Any fruits? Been around animals or livestock? Have you traveled to the land of the coronavirus during the last two weeks? And then came the punch in the kisser: "reason for visit."

Thankfully, someone had taken the liberty of saving all passengers the time and the agony of having to write out the commonest answers to this question—this[4] may have well been a question on *Family Feud*. You can just hear Steve Harvey saying,[5] "With the scores tied, we now go to sudden death. Only the top three answers on the board. We surveyed one hundred people in the audience. We want to know, what is a reason you might go to Hawaii?"

1. Wedding Proposal
2. Honeymoon
3. Anniversary

Somewhere after "Independent Study of Marine Biology" and "Sporting Event," you found the generic "Tourism" bubble and filled it in. Because you had already leaned into the whole *Sarah Marshall*[6] motif, you found this amusing and stored this data in a file titled "Self-Fulfilling Prophecies," where it fit quite nicely. You also couldn't help but chortle at the thought of someone trying to nervously hide their answers from their unsuspecting partner while bubbling in #1. *This is going to be a good trip*, you reconcile in that moment.

Although you had neither been dating a TV star nor been burning her pictures on the stove, you were in pretty rough shape. Psychologically, you were in a pretty similar rebound state as Pete, but your execution was as fruitless as his was comedic.

2. Uncanny but admittedly limited similarities. Readers familiar with Mr. Segel's magnum opus will likely recollect an infamous scene wherein the protagonist displays full frontal nudity, an apt metaphor for a relationship. This present work adheres exclusively to metaphorical nudity and contains no graphic representation of genitalia of any sort. You may be relieved or disappointed as you wish.

3. The most uniquely *homo sapien* of all traits.

4. Three cheers for the em dash!

5. Richard Karn or Louie Anderson would also work. But truth be told, John O'Hurley would always be to *Family Feud* what Bob Barker is to *The Price Is Right* in your mind. No offense, Drew Carey.

6. Watching *Forgetting Sarah Marshall* was a prerequisite for reading this book. Did you not read the syllabus?

At least you didn't have to endure Billy Baldwin's one-liners from *Crime Scene: Scene of the Crime* reruns over the Pacific. Cue the wildly inappropriate *Seinfeld*-esque music.

Your two most recent exes remained stateside, but both would be texting you in the next forty-eight hours. Had you not already been in the headspace of rehashing relationships past, this may have seriously upset the flow of your trip, but as it stood, these outreaches would only fuel your creative process.

Whereas Jason Segel's Bretter[7] was working on *A Taste for Love,* you had been channeling some of your lifetime of good damage by taking pen to the page. Part therapy, part drunken dare to write extensively in the second person, you were trudging through the quagmire of romances long expired for a publishable narrative. You hoped to strike the same heartfelt but comedic balance as your favorite vampire-themed puppet musical. And in the vein of the play on words that humanized Dracula in Bretter's title, you searched for a title to similarly capture the essence of humor and heart. That film was a true embodiment of the aphorism that comedy is tragedy plus time. Relying, then, on some algebraic sleight of hand, you supposed your story would be one of comedy minus time.[8] Not forsaking the funny parts, but still, at its core, about a set of perceived tragedies, you had the crux of your title: *Comedy Minus Time.* The misadventures in romance, marginal comments, and non sequiturs would come later in the writing process.

7.   Fun aside: you once recommended this film to a dear friend but did not want to spoil the brilliance of the nude scene. In her blissful ignorance, she decided to rent and watch it with her parents, explicitly citing you as the referring source. None of you has ever made comfortable eye contact since, including at your friend's wedding.

8.   You sincerely hope that your high school English teachers read this title and at least crack a bemused smile.

1

BAD SELF PORTRAITS[ii]

The first page of the first chapter of the first volume in your failed romances begins, accordingly, in the first grade. It happens when a classmate plants your first kiss squarely on your cheek.[9]

You tell on her, not so much to get her in trouble[10] but because you aren't sure what else to do. When the lunchroom staff inquires whether you wanted her to kiss you, you *really* aren't sure what to do.

Imparted with all the knowledge, wisdom, and life experience afforded to you by reaching the third grade, you attempt to dive into your next nonplatonic endeavor. After confiding your

9. For some ungodly reason, your mother has still saved to this very day a handful of notes this girl wrote to you. Even well into your adulthood, you have been known to wryly remark that you peaked early romantically, but a vague whiff of truth haunts this self-deprecating joke. Your first kiss moved away, and you've never heard from or seen her again.

Fun bonus comment, you thought the phrase "self-defecating" humor was correct usage for well into your twenties.

10. Disciplinary action in the form of a mark was standard retribution for unwanted physical contact (i.e., pushing or shoving), and you supposed that this fit neatly into that set of rules.

11. By "friend," you mean someone who sat near you in grade school and also happened to enjoy playing King's Quest V and VI. 1993 was a much simpler time.

12. To paraphrase Winston Churchill, this is the type of arrant pedantry up with which you, the reader, will have to put.

13. While you don't remember the first time your mom drove you to a platonic, all-boys gathering, these words live verbatim in your memory.

feelings to a male friend[11] you thought you could trust, the little rat goes and spills the beans of your affection directly to the girl you kind of like. When she confronts you regarding these alleged feelings, you deny everything and use the memorable phrase "why that little …" in describing your friend to this girl. In recanting your affection, you inevitably say things that hurt her feelings because she just thought you liked her—and she probably liked you a little bit too. But alas, there is no joy in Mudville this day. And fortunately for you, there are no real consequences for your actions. But, there is no real breakup because there is nothing up from which to break.[12]

───────

Through the fifth grade, you are not particularly popular, electing instead to focus your efforts and energies on the rigors of a public elementary school education at the expense of popularity (not that you have much of a choice in the matter). You ascend to the middle school level of education before anyone invites you to hang out independently of a school or athletic function.

In fact, you reach eighth grade before attending a social gathering with members of both sexes. Since you're too young to drive yourself, your mother chauffeurs you to the party. As she pulls into a parking space, she slowly turns around from the driver's seat and solemnly advises you and your brother:

"No means no means no."[13]

The brevity of this statement stems from a crippling inability-turned-family-practice to have deep conversations regarding any topic of any real import.[14]

In many ways, your parents are gender prototypes frozen in time from the 1950s. Your father fancies himself a hybrid of Robert Young's titular patriarch from *Father Knows Best* and Tim Allen's Mike Baxter from *Last Man Standing*.[15] Indispensable as much as he felt infallible, Dad's viewpoints aren't so much perspectives as they are objective truths in his eyes. Mom, on the other hand, could have filled in on set as June Cleaver without ever reading a script or stage notes. Near as you can tell, she has grown to dutifully accept this role more than enjoying it exactly—a fate less unique to her and more a symptom of prevailing social norms with which your parents govern their lives and yours.[16]

You wish your mother had issued these words, to have known their meaning just a few short years prior to her pre-party warning. If you had possessed the syntax of verbal sanctuary at that time, then perhaps you could have used them in your defense. But it was too late. Your mother's assessment that you would be an aggressor was tragically misplaced, and instead, you were more likely to have benefited from using her words as a shield rather than channeling ugly patriarchy to dismiss them in pursuit of sexual conquest.

Night has fallen and covered the landscape with an anonymity afforded only by darkness. Given your generally strict upbringing, one of the most enjoyable consequences of spending a night outside of your home is the opportunity to stay up past your bedtime of 8:00 p.m. sharp. It also means that on nights spent elsewhere, you are intoxicated with the slaphappiness of fatigue when the hour hand of the clock encroaches on delirium.

On this particular night, you are introduced to a game called "Truth or Dare."[17] Initially scared of the *dare* category, you opt instead to answer questions (mostly) truthfully about yourself to fall in line with the norms of the game. But the waning hours of the night act as alcohol on your prepubescent mind, lowering your inhibitions in favor of curiosity.

14. The two seconds it takes her to issue this stern warning served as one of two sex talks you ever received from your parents. This talk was preemptive, but the other was in direct response to the unexpected nature of the arrival of your little brother, eleven years your junior. Despite a tubal ligation, your mother had become pregnant with the newest member of the family, an event that your parents deemed worthy of an explanation. To borrow from Jeff Goldblum's Ian Malcom, "Life, uh, finds a way."

15. These programs bookended a perfect day by your dad's estimate. A full hour of postwar situational comedy resolved by fatherly cunning punctuated by "viral" rants on conservative talking points? All from the comfort of the couch? Heaven may well be a place on earth.

16. Years later, you wonder how they each would have turned out differently if your dad hadn't proposed to your mom after three months of dating.

17. In your experience, this game is particularly well suited for those who have adequate social lubrication. But those without power are vulnerable to unwillingly fall prey to empowered and opportunistic participants, whether drunk or not.

You are selected by someone older—someone you very much look up to and trust. Despite being nearly incapable of emotional expression, you had explicitly told him you loved him, although you meant it platonically. You believed he had reciprocated the feeling, but the sentiment of your words had yet to echo back. Instead, you find yourself at the mercy of his suggestion, unsupervised in a basement.

When you choose *truth*, the questions he asks are sexual in nature. Your innocence and lack of knowledge on the topics are plain as day, yet they do not detract from a barrage of physiology and anatomy lessons. You frequently ask clarifying questions to ascertain some understanding about what certain verbs mean, what body parts look like, and for slang to be translated into words you can understand. Your sexual ignorance proves to be a mere speed bump in the inevitable journey forward rather than a stop sign or exit ramp. Perhaps your naivety is even a preference in his eyes.

To begin with,[18] you are told that you should not view "private parts"[19] as dirty, bad, or even private. In fact, you ought to consider them just like any other body part—as an elbow, for instance.[20] During one such sexual explanation,[21] you are supposed to truthfully answer which of your aunts you find the most attractive.[22]

By night's end, you are never put in physical pain, and you don't feel as though you are in danger any of the times this happens.

I hate you for what you did
And I miss you like a little kid

Another year passes before your elementary school guidance counselor enlightens your fifth-grade class about the dangers of

---

18. Having spent every single day of the past quarter century repressing these memories, trying to contain them in an airtight box in the corner of your mind, concrete details elude your mental grasp, but a few specifics remain intact.

19. As you were wont to call them at an age before being introduced to the myriad lexicon of phallic euphemisms, and before you were mature enough to even use the word *penis*.

20. In retrospect, you now know that you were being coaxed and groomed to perform sexual tasks, but at the time, you took it as a face-value assertion that you were being wrong-minded in your conceptualization of sexuality. You had much to learn and an all-too-willing teacher.

21. Or "sexplanation," if you will. You're not above using portmanteau mid-reveal of your most painful memories. After all, humor has been an oft-effective defense mechanism throughout your life.

22. This was the diluted question, anyway, considering you didn't, at age ten, truly comprehend what "to have sex with" entailed, even after it had been explained to you.

revealing areas covered by your swimsuits—an apt public school vernacular proxy for "sex organs." These presentations warn you to exercise caution, even among people you know and trust, but this warning comes too late to preserve your innocence. As the guidance counselor talks, you feel uncomfortable, but at a level dwarfed by the real experience. You hope you are the only one among your peers who has had previous experience from which to draw. Unfortunately, you know that hope would fall flat in the face of facts.

> *I have emotional motion sickness*
> *Somebody roll the window down*

Before shutting down all thoughts related to the Truth or Dare night, you begin to wonder if you were merely a vehicle for sexual pleasure. Your aggressor had a physical, lusting desire, and you were the closest outlet capable of satisfying his desire. Because you admire and want this person to value you and love you back, your brain steers you along the path of complicity and silence, as requested by your perpetrator. He had the knowledge of foresight that if your secret got out to anyone, ever, he would be in a lot of trouble. Whether he knew it or not (and you believe he did), he exercised a tremendous amount of power over you on account of your imbalanced emotional ledger. At the time, you understood none of this, however. Numbness fills in admirably for the place where one might expect pain to have occupied your brain.[23]

Despite your sheltered and conservative upbringing, your first sexual experiences are with another male.[24] You don't think of these acts as homosexual because, despite only male sex organs being involved, no feelings of love or emotional desire enter into the equation. These aforementioned incidents, however, lead you to aggressively condemn male–male relations for years to come. Such disdain comes less from moral qualms and more from your desire to not be found out and subjected to the

23. Looking back, you suspect that the human brain is uniquely adapted to promote self-preservation. Many years later, you will badly break your ankle and also feel no pain; it's as if your central nervous system is intimately aware of the stress and pain you can take and knows to shut down the nerve endings to the afflicted area, whether it be an ankle or the part of your brain associated with traumatic experiences.

24. The first time you would admit to being sexually abused to someone other than a therapist came shortly after Dr. Blasey Ford's testimony against Brett Kavanaugh. A sexually assertive, bordering-on-aggressive male friend of yours openly questioned why she waited so long to tell her story. Like word vomit, you blurted out that, as a survivor yourself, memories of the events haunt you every day. You were asked to keep the encounters a secret because, if you ever told anyone, this person you admired and trusted would get in trouble. And you didn't want that, did you? Your friend could not have understood the power of binding pacts formed in sexual secret.

ridicule that a jury of your peers would use upon finding you guilty of being different. To be considered gay in your school system at this time of your life would be social ruination.[25] It's a lot to consider, especially at a time when you are still receiving X-Men action figures as birthday presents.

There are no words in the English language
I could scream to drown you out[iii]

———

Your middle school years are characterized by your peers exuding awkward, wholly unwarranted confidence and bravado. This results in classmates obeying social norms and their libidos, starting relationships with the opposite sex for the first time. Their prevailing wisdom responsible for initiating relationships (consistent with the hallmark brain physiology of puberty) is usually along the lines of "This chick in my class has big boobs." Captain Nemo's *Nautilus* should aspire to such depth.

Faking it in hopes of reaching the proverbial "making it" phase, you begin your search for a girl to date. You meet your first crush, who reciprocates precisely none of the feelings you have for her. But she is a nice girl and a good sport, so she indulges you by graciously agreeing to attend a few dances and sock hops together.[26]

At the first such dance, you work yourself up to the point of psychosomatic digestive distress, when suddenly you hear the first few notes of a highly recognizable slow song. You convince yourself it's your duty[27] to power through your discomfort and anxiety to get out there and dance with her. You emerge from the bathroom[28] by your locker (#14, combination 8-44-12) and make a beeline for your date.

Baby, when you touch me,
I can feel how much you love me[29]

25.   A victim though you were, you were privileged to go on living your life, dating who you wanted to, without fear of being relegated as an outcast. Not everyone is blessed with that option in the face of hate and lack of understanding.

26.   In a rare demonstration of self-worth, you will eventually take umbrage when she confides to a mutual friend, "If no one wants to date me, I guess I'll just date him."

27.   Double entendre alert!

28.   Totally worth it!

29.   These have to be the first draft lyrics written on a napkin. Touch and love are lazy near-rhymes. You're a professional—write like it, dammit!

She's radiant! She's perfect! She's the one, and it all started right here, on the baseline of your middle school gym! She's … got really long arms, so the chaperones aren't going to yell at us for being too close! Awesome!

Wow. Look at how great her hair is! Some of it is covering her forehead. What are those called? Bangs? Yeah, you like her bangs. And her smile. Wait, why isn't she smiling? Is she not as into this as you are?

> *I've never been this close*
> *To anyone, or anything.*
> *I can hear your thoughts,*
> *I can see your dreams*[30]

Aw, shit—here comes the good part! Treasure this moment forever! This is the greatest moment of your young life—you're convinced of it! It has to be! And to think, this moment, right now, a few feet from the free throw line in your middle school gym…

> *Every little thing that you do,*[31]
> *Baby, I'm amazed by you*[iv]

Despite the now-obvious signs First Crush is clearly not interested in you as a permanent dance partner, let alone a long-term, monogamous companion, you try to dance to every single slow song with her. Every. Single. One. Because that's what you're supposed to do—right?

––––––––––

You wish this were the only dance where you face guarded this poor girl, but that would be horribly misremembering the facts. At some point, she attempts to persuade you that you don't have to dance[32] with her for every single song. During one such

30.   The already weak rhyme scheme jig is up. Also, this sounds like Bill Walton announcing a basketball game.

31.   This is so dumb, vague, and generic that it needs The Roots and Steve Higgins to try to make it palatable.

32.   *Dance*, when used as a verb, will refer to slow dancing unless otherwise specified. In seventh grade, you lacked the rhythm and confidence to move your body in space without specific instructions and explicit protocol for acceptable dance moves. Grinding would be strictly forbidden for another year, leaving you to complain about the pop music selection during non-slow songs.

33. This was "your song" with the girl you would go on to date in eighth grade. You vividly recall waiting in line with your future sister-in-law to request it at the Farewell Dance. She opted to request Creed's "With Arms Wide Open," although neither would be played. The overly raucous group reaction to the playing of "Chop Suey!" from the request list ensured no more student selections would be heard that night.

34. Gosh, it's good to be a beta. Alphas have to work so frightfully hard...

event, some girl intercepts you as you are en route toward your preferred dance partner.

She is one of those popular, attractive girls, which immediately instills the sense that something is amiss. You are baffled to find yourself within arms' reach of her, much less at a length where your arms aren't awkwardly outstretched to ward off chaperone suspicion. While *she* had approached *you* to dance, her face gives you the distinct impression she is having precisely no fun. Neither of you speaks a word to the other during the dance or after she disengages and walks away at the conclusion of KC and JoJo's "All My Life"[33] or whatever cheesy song has just finished playing.

But being the consummate scab picker that you are, you feel compelled to find out more. One night, you fire up the internet and log into AOL Instant Messenger. For some reason, the gods of middle school hierarchies[34] have deemed you worthy of possessing the screen name of this popular, attractive girl who danced a little too close for your comfort. You send a message to her, painfully aware you are reaching across the void between the two social strata.

Without so much as a "How do you do?" you launch into an unexpected inquisition of why she danced with you, why she was dancing so closely, and whether or not this was the result of her having lost a bet. Your social ineptitude leads you to ask more questions befitting of a stranger in a strange land, a la Brendan Fraser's protagonist in *Blast from the Past*. Such a line of questioning is off-putting enough that she immediately gets offline or blocks you. Either way, the conversation is punctuated with the sound of a digital door closing. You will never again speak, virtually or verbally, to your interceptor again.

Unsettled and unsatisfied with your lack of understanding social norms, your suspicions point toward the theory that you were being used as a vehicle of social embarrassment. Perhaps she was demonstrating she could dance with anyone she wanted. Perhaps one of her friends had dared her to do it for sport. Perhaps she did it as a favor to her friend, First Crush—distracting you so that her friend could enjoy dancing with someone else who wasn't such a social dullard and so damned territorial.[35]

———

Evidently, some of the wholly unwarranted and awkward bravado common among your testosterone-ridden peers has rubbed off on you. Or at least their brazen horniness has.

There's this girl in your English class, also on the cheer squad. Cheerleader has boobs—ergo, you like her and decide you want to ask her out. Before taking this plunge, though, you assess your chances by talking to one of her friends, who happens to be your twin brother's girlfriend, already going on one year[36] by eighth grade.

The mutual connection breaks the news to your boob-having new crush. You still remember what she says, verbatim, when you approach her at her locker to ask her out.

"I've decided to say yes."[37]

But you dive in, headfirst, to the shallow end of this pool. Despite the somber tone of her voice, her strained and distant posture, and the actual words that came out of her mouth, you act like she welcomed you with arms wide open.

You're waiting for someone
To put you together[38]

She is a cheerleader, in honors classes, and thereby, you calculate, popular. This will have to reflect well on you—dating someone of this social stature.

Christmas is right around the corner—you need to get her something. Your family is going to Disney in a week or two

35.   You only develop this final hypothesis a solid eighteen years after the fact, when everyone else in the story was married, many with children.

36.   If memory serves, you believe they finished second or third for cutest couple in the eighth-grade superlative voting. Having already been an item for a year by the time of the vote certainly helped their case.

37.   The civil engineers at Pompeii had fewer red flags.

38.   While researching the lyrics to this seventh-grade jam, you see an advertisement for "Now That's What I Call the 1990s" and wonder who, in 2020, would purchase a physical copy of this album. Obviously someone has; you just want to know who.

for AAU Cross Country Nationals. Maybe you should pick up something for her there—an ornament would be festive! But will that be enough?

> *He's everything you want*
> *He's everything you need*[39]

She'd better be ready for this, because all the men in your family lock it down. Your cousin has been dating his girlfriend for two years already. Your brother and his girlfriend are going on a year, and your dad married your mom after like three months of dating.

> *I say all the right things*
> *At exactly the right time*
> *But I mean nothing to you*
> *And I don't know why*[v]

During Christmastime, you tie up the phone line for the better part of an hour[40] trying to find the lyrics to Jose Feliciano's classic, "Feliz Navidad," and wait for Cheerleader to get on AOL instant messenger so you can type the lyrics out to her. You elect not to copy and paste, not from a lack of shortcut key command but because the labor of typing it out seemed more heartfelt to you. Plus the lyrics include the phrase "from the bottom of my heart," which is the organ most associated with love, so you know, it's mushy stuff all girls are programmed to love, and you reckon[41] she would really appreciate the sentiment and the trouble. Cheerleader does not. Just because you have two reasons for wanting to date her doesn't mean she has any reasons for wanting to keep dating you.[42]

39. You remember wanting to form a cover band called Horizontal Vertices. Somehow that idea never really took off.

40. Future generations will never know the crippling inconvenience of having to use telephonic infrastructure to use the internet. The inconvenience nearly turned everyone into a Karen.

41. Is "reckon" shorthand for "reconcile" in this context? It certainly seems to fit.

42. This relationship was so short-lived that it didn't even make the first draft of this manuscript. Whoops!

2

ERA VULGARIS[vi]

You have moved on from suffocating Cheerleader and First Crush, and have become a weighted blanket to a cross country teammate of the latter ex. The transition from seventh to eighth grade has imbued within you the smallest possible incremental interpersonal progress, and you coolly give it time before stress testing her windpipe with your neediness.

Starting high school with a girlfriend already in tow has made you feel accomplished and helps you settle into what pop culture has you believe is a planet with an entirely different atmospheric composition than middle school. You find this to be

43.   You work the term *girlfriend* into conversations with the same voracity as someone who does CrossFit talks about their WOD. And yes, it is just as annoying.

44. You forsake a basic statistical analysis of this claim. Even if it were possible to distill love into an algorithm, the likelihood that the singular person whose constellation of personality and preferences most clearly matches your needs just so happens to live in the same town of twelve thousand people as you at the exact same time … is small. Like, having your perfect NCAA basketball bracket get struck by lightning small.

45. Fun future fact: the first time you perform cunnilingus, you will become sick to your stomach. When you reveal this to a future girlfriend, she will find it uproariously funny, while you take yourself far too seriously to enjoy the honest-to-god hilarity of the story.

mostly untrue, but having a relationship on the "solved" side of the ledger gives you peace of mind. And things are going well in this regard, according to your preconceived rubric for how relationships can go. In fact, you exhibit a rare demonstration of public affection and vulnerability toward your own girlfriend.[43]

It happens in your fourth-period health class—the teacher asks if anyone thinks there is exactly one perfect person[44] meant for everyone. You raise your hand. The follow-up question comes: who thinks they've already found that person? Your hand remains in the air. You do this, in part, because you think it true but also because two of her teammates are both in the room and are likely to report back to said girlfriend about the sweet thing you did, publicly. With any luck, you can parlay those brownie points into some mouth stuff.[45]

The physical aspect of your relationship benefits greatly due to the fact that your girlfriend is the youngest of three and is generally well behaved. This allows her mother to trust her when you come over, instead focusing her attention on the habitually mischievous middle child. Furthermore, her dad is essentially out of the picture.

Her parents aren't separated, but her dad is an alcoholic—not the fun type you see in movies and on sitcoms whose hijinks are zany and harmless, but the crippling type whose daughter you date for two years, and you only ever speak six or seven words to him. No, he's the type of drunk who, after working at the steel mill all day, spends more of his conscious time at a bar than with his family, only coming home when his BAC electromagnetically affixes him to the couch in front of his TV. Imagine Gilbert Grape's mother, replace her obesity with alcoholism, and you get a sense of his contribution to the family dynamic. The railroad tracks you cross getting to her part of town bring you– both literally and figuratively– to the wrong side of the tracks.

But you don't mind, or really even notice it at the time,

because you are a teenage boy whose libido is at the wheel.[46] As such, your parents (and her mother) take turns hauling your asses around to go on dates, the first of which is to go see *Spider-Man*[47] in theaters. You drop the L word on Ms. Grape for the first time as Tobey McGuire dangles upside down on the silver screen, locking lips with Kirsten Dunst. Having seen this scene in previews, you execute your premeditated plan by leaning over and telling her you love her. This seven-layer cliché dip is much to her liking, which regrettably will serve as a blueprint for your romantic gestures longer than you will be proud to admit. But in the present moment, it's like shooting fish in a barrel, and you're following the relationship rules in accordance with trite pop culture tropes. So you get a free pass for now because navigating adolescence is a punishing minefield of determining the extent to which you want to belong or retain your own distinct personality. That is, if you even find it during these years.

──────────

Your first foray into the land of vulnerability occurs in this first relationship. Well, your first opportunity to do so, anyway. As the chance to express empathy presents itself, you stomp on it and snuff it out as though your homeroom teacher were about to catch you sneaking a Pall Mall behind the dumpster.

Against all odds, the two of you find a spare minute between using your mouths for other things to discuss details about pre-race strategies. Ms. Grape mentions needing to take a shower to wash off even the last speck of dirt that might weigh her down.[48] You guffaw, projecting ballistic spittle[49] in her general direction. Whatever your verbal reply, it embodies the same sentiment. And despite your inability to demonstrate any helpful opinion or emotion, she continues, explaining how she feels compelled to tie her shoes a very particular way and to turn her lights off

46. A curious metaphor, because at fourteen years of age, you are not yet old enough to drive.

47. The first incarnation, before Marvel reboots happened seemingly mid-film.

48. Mamas, don't let your babies grow up to be distance runners. The razor-thin line between balancing body weight with having an eating disorder cuts a tragic number of these athletes. Mindlessly blurting out platitudes in the vein of "You look like you could use a cheeseburger" do not help. Be kind.

49. During a particularly brilliant stand-up set, Demetri Martin describes sneaking increasingly ludicrous words and phrases into answers during his miserable time at law school. This seems like one of those sentences but is surprisingly not!

a certain number of times before leaving the room. In the days predating WebMD, she had painstakingly researched and diagnosed herself with obsessive compulsive disorder. Only at this point do you start to grasp the gravity of the situation, realizing she needs you to exhibit a different emotion. You plunge into waters unknown. It's the belly of all flops.

After a moment of mulling, you conclude that the most heartfelt, loving thing you can do is tell Ms. Grape you don't believe in OCD. She is perfect the way she is, and a diagnosis like that would mean there was something wrong with her. Not on your fifteen-year-old watch. This is what passes as romance in your wretchedly misguided perception of mental health and of relationships. Realizing your folly, you deftly maneuver and redirect your oral efforts into less noble pursuits to demonstrate caring another way.

I wrote her off for the tenth time today[50]
Practiced all the things I would say
She came over, I lost my nerve
I took her back and made her dessert

This is Conflict Resolution 101 for the two of you, and you can't argue[51] with the short-term results.

I know I should say no
It's kind of hard when she's ready to go
I might be dumb, but I'm not a dweeb
I'm just a sucker with no self esteem[vii]

Because you are, in many ways, a rather faithful carbon copy of your father, it turns out that you are a lousy boyfriend, and Ms. Grape leaves you for some other guy. Word on the street is that he is well endowed, and you assume she is only interested in this aspect of him. You think about and feel like calling her

50. In about fifteen years, a dear friend of yours will sing this song at karaoke, and the performance will be completely indistinguishable from the Offspring's studio version ... for the first five seconds of the track.

51. Your tongue was tied, thereby rendering you incapable of argument.

any number of sexually charged, derogatory names but never muster the gall to do so. Because you are also a rather faithful carbon copy of your mother, you internalize the pain, keep your feelings to yourself, and trust only yourself to disarm the emotional bomb that will inevitably go off.

Another transfer from your maternal carbon paper may best be described by chancellor Adam Sutler from the dystopian *V for Vendetta.* After the breakup, you feel "buried under the avalanche of your inadequacies," emotional evidence that sets a precedent for all breakups in your near to mid future. Like *Pygmalion in the Classroom,*[52] you have begun what you do not yet realize is a self-fulfilling prophecy[53] of anguish.[54]

———

For the next two years, you believe in a narrow band of meritocracy: good things are supposed to happen to good people. To this end, you act the part of what you think a good person ought to be—studious[55] in the classroom and industrious[56] on the track. But for some reason, these traits do not win you the favor of females. You feel entitled to some modicum of admiration, if not outright adulation, because you consider yourself to be smart and a good athlete. You *deserve* to be loved, and you contend that love should come from a girl who is just as smart and whose physical beauty eclipses your own level of attractiveness. You know, because that's fair.[57]

So in the tradition of the Germanic Goths of the sixteenth century, you go off to club a girl over the head to make her your own. Luckily, just such a girl exists, and you happen to know exactly how to play this one cool. You look up her phone number in the telephone book, pick up a corded telephone, and, in a very unsolicited and unsuspecting manner, call her parents' house. After the niceties of a formal greeting, you launch into

52. You could just say "self-fulfilling prophecy" but have convinced yourself to refer to a somewhat obscure reference to an article you once read for class as an undergraduate. Shout-out to Dr. Vealey, if you're reading this!

53. R. Rosenthal and Lenore Jacobson, "Pygmalion in the Classroom," *Urban Review* (1965): 16-20.

54. You will later lament that a relationship based on so little, which started at so young an age, was one of your longest-lasting, even into your mid-thirties. Of course, you know that longevity does not equate to a successful relationship, whatever definition of the word success. Although your parents' marriage painfully proves this point, the next twenty years of being romantically underemployed will play some tricks with your head.

55. A very deliberate word choice. You are not smart, not yet. Intelligence is derived from critical thinking skills, of which you currently have none. You have been trained to memorize and regurgitate state-standard materials, and your near-4.0 GPA has little to do with real, meaningful smarts.

56.   It would kill you, circa 2005, to read these words today, but the percentage of your athletic prowess attributable to hard work is merely the tip of the iceberg. You won the genetic jackpot and are virtually predestined to succeed in long-distance aerobic activities.

57.   Thanks, *According to Jim*!

58.   Maladroit (adj.)— ineffective or bungling; clumsy. See also: Criminally *Underrated Weezer Albums*, 1 entry.

59.   Quoting obscure lines from popular TV shows and movies is a completely useless passion of yours. This little number was from Frank Capra's *It's a Wonderful Life*.

60.   Come to think of it, you will remember her birthday fifteen years after the fact on account of that screen name, you creepy Rain Man.

a conversation as though there were some sensible pretext for doing so. Even more luckily for you, she doesn't immediately hang up the receiver in response to you stumbling through your maladroit[58] talking points. You don't know it at the time, but she has a boyfriend. When you do discover this information, you do not change your course, because that would be so not Goth. "To the victor go the spoils," "may the best man win," and other misused aphorisms will fill your head in an attempt to justify your rotten behavior and level of entitlement.

Because her boyfriend is a senior, and the two of you are juniors, he will eventually be out of the picture, and your slow play pays off. It's a foregone conclusion that she will immediately fall in love with you because her former flame is now Old Joe College.[59] The possibility of them staying together in a long-distance relationship never even enters your mind.

Rather than having karma spite your hubris, the two of you do date. These are the glory days. You work on precalculus homework together, checking your answers against each other. Luckily she lives in such close proximity that you can start driving back three minutes before curfew and still sneak in on time. She is both the literal and figurative Girl Next Door.

You miss recruiting phone calls from college cross country coaches because you are at her house and don't yet have a cell phone. The two of you have a magnificent pillow-fight-turned-tickle-fight, of which you are clearly the victor. You go on easy Sunday-morning runs together. You hold hands in public for the first time as the youngest couple watching *Walk the Line* in theaters. You even ride a goddamned tandem bicycle together. You tie up the phone line waiting for her to sign onto AOL instant messenger[60] and send her a message every time you see her screen name pop up, because you have no chill. But she likes you despite all this, so life is good.

You try to downplay the importance of going to the

homecoming dance, admonishing peers who care so much about it that they make it a big deal. But one week later, with foot firmly in mouth, you ask her to the dance. When you find out she will be wearing a brown dress, your mother immediately goes out to buy you a shirt she believes will match.[61]

Perhaps the most prominent differences between middle school and high school are related to acceptable physical contact between students. Once upon a time, you and Ms. Grape had gotten busted for making out in a dark hallway[62] and sent to the vice principal's office, but just three short years later, the high school dance could easily be described as flash mob dry humping set to music. And despite being generally opposed to activities of mass popularity, you do begrudgingly dance. You and the Girl Next Door take to the dance floor upon hearing the first note of arguably the most played song at events of this type.

> *Baby when we're grinding*
> *I get so excited*

You, in inadvertent armchair cosplay, just try to match the way she's moving her body. The lack of rigorous, step-by-step instructions and a clear right way to do things causes you mild anxiety—not enough to make you stop, just enough to make you self-conscious.

> *Oooh, how I like it*
> *I try but I can't hide it*[63]

Damn her for being five foot four. You don't know if you can get that low, but you're happy to oblige …

> *Oh, you're dancing real close*
> *'cause it's real, real slow*

You only understand like a third of the words in this song

61. Photographic evidence suggests that while she looked like an aspiring model, you more nearly resembled a sofa that had fallen into disrepair.

62. Quoting obscure lines from nineties rock songs is another pointless passion. See if you can find them all hidden in this text!

63. Say what you will, but this is good use of near rhyme, internal rhyme, and assonance. Way better than that Lonestar BS from the seventh-grade dance.

but really like how the female vocalist on the track hits the high note on the last part. You remember hearing that NASA had paid people to send them their sweat for research purposes. If this were true, today you could be responsible for five percent of their total spending budget. Is your sweat off-putting to her, or does she even notice?

You're making it hard[64] for me[viii]

After the concert at the sauna ends, you retreat to the basement of The House Next Door. You've actually been here many years ago; your dad helped build the house and brought you, a preschooler, along to help. You vaguely remember standing in their basement at four years of age, not terribly far from where you are right now, albeit for a very different purpose. All that gyrating, getting low, and sweating has necessitated a wardrobe change.[65]

———

You don't break up so much as dissolve. There is no precipitating argument, no burnout, just a slow fade away. This is partly because there was never much in the way of a real relationship. You did flirt with her in your awkward nerd-speak,[66] but you never risked any depth, any vulnerability. You were doing an impression of a 1950s-era, dime-a-dozen male placeholder who would have brought Norman Rockwell to tears. Maybe that's why she's the one who got away—you never gave the Girl Next Door anything uniquely yours, for fear she might not understand or appreciate it.[67]

———

64. Hard for me to do what, exac—Oh. Oh shit. Mr. Goetz definitely didn't vet this DJ or song.

65. You ask to borrow a shirt, which you "accidentally" forget to give back for years. It will make its way with you to at least two different dorm rooms in undergrad before being returned to its rightful owner, despite your parents living literally one kilometer away from hers. Maybe you kept it as a trophy, maybe as a memento of a time you never thought you could replicate.

66. "Be pneumatic for Ford's sake!" was hardly flattering when you wrote it in her binder during the Brave New World unit, and it would be even less so today.

67. In your defense, though, you were just an eighteen-year-old kid who didn't know a damn thing about life outside of the experiences of the twelve thousand people in your hometown. How could you define yourself as an individual when your life had been heretofore defined by your participation on teams or as a member of a family?

The doldrum months of winter drudge on after the crisp, autumnal cross country season. You find respite filling in for the high school radio station nerds who usually announce the high school basketball games. Unsure of how you got the gig, but grateful they approached you, you promptly clear your already-open Friday-evening schedule to call a ball game.

Before the game starts,[68] a loosely connected acquaintance tells you that one of her friends wants to talk to you on behalf of a third friend[69] who might want to ask you out. An interesting proposition, you figure, but a la Aaron Samuels at Chris Eisel's Halloween party, you end up with the messenger rather than the actual interested party. Unlike Aaron Samuels, you initiate this hijacking. On a related note, you have recently been introduced to the movie *Mean Girls*,[70] and against every fiber of your hegemonically masculine sensibility and every preconceived notion about a movie with a female lead ensemble, you absolutely love it.

Out of guilt, embarrassment, or just plain old astonishment, Ms. Messenger agrees to date you. You reward this undeserved, blind confidence with an invitation for your first date to be at your little brother's birthday party, in front of your entire family. Your first date.

With the patience of a saint, this poor girl endures the party and an additional two more weeks of your auto-neurotic asphyxiation. Were she a rabbit, Lenny would find your embrace excessive. When Valentine's Day arrives, you administer the ultimate squeeze on the relationship.

You've got the most unbelievable blue eyes I've ever seen
You've got me almost melting away

Engaging in the time-honored performance of obligatory romantic posturing, you patronize the seasonal aisle of the supermarket after all the top-tier bullshit consumables have been

68. A quick sidenote on the athletic proceedings. You were assigned to a two-man crew to call the game, and your partner does not say a word—you get Vin Scullied against your will, in your first-ever foray into commentary. No matter how many times you tried to prompt your color commentator for an opinion, statistic, or anecdote, he remained wordless. That was some real bullshit, Brian...

69. We've already used up half of our moves to get to Kevin Bacon and haven't left the same homeroom class. Woof.

70. When it comes to movie quotes and useless music trivia, your memory is crystalline, and *Mean Girls* is the Crown Jewel of your eidetic pop culture memory.

71.   In 2019, you will earn the nickname "Mudge"— doubly truncated from "curmudgeon." The name aptly described you long before the moniker was actually bestowed upon you.

picked through. The purpose of pleasing your partner pales in comparison to the true meaning of the holiday—peddling card-stock platitudes and diabetes-by-the-bite to exceed projections for the Q1 goals. And you buy right into it, like the consumerist sheep you have been trained to be.[71]

I love you, always forever
Near and far, close and together

You show up at Ms. Messenger's locker, heart-shaped box obscured behind your back. She accepts the token but can't continue dating you. Although you're a nice person, a good student, and a good athlete, you don't have anything in common. Rather than admit she's right, you simply implore her to give you more time, to train on the job, as it were. But because she's a reasonable person, she sticks to her guns, making you feel hung out to dry. There are lessons to be learned from this experience, but today is not the day you learn them. Instead, you flip on the radio, feeling alone and underappreciated.

Everywhere I will be with you
Everything I will do for you[ix]

72.   Years later, you will remember thinking that women the world over were missing out on how great you are. At one point, you wondered, hypothetically, if you took yourself off the dating market, who would really be worse off for it—you or the collective of womankind for not seeing your greatness. Thankfully, your *Atlas Shrugged* phase would not be very long-lived.

After your inevitable breakup, the country music station on your presets blares:

Well ask anybody, I'm a pretty good guy,
And the looks decent wagon didn't pass me by[72]
There ain't nothin' in my past that I'm tryin' hard to hide
And I don't understand why I gotta wonder why

This guy totally gets it. What more do you have to do to get a girl? You've done all the things you've been told to do and checked all the eligible bachelor boxes, so what gives?

> *What's a guy gotta do to get a girl in this town?*
> *Don't wanna be alone when the sun goes down*
> *Just a sweet little somethin' to put my arms around*
> *What's a guy gotta do to get a girl in this town?*[x]

Preach. This song perfectly captures the frustration of being a single boy in high school—especially one who is a consummate rule follower and confused as to why he's acing his classes but failing in romantic relationships.

———

Your best friend on the cross country team is one of those popular, attractive guys who is so cool that he has invited friends from other high schools over to his house for a party.[73] Word spreads, and two girls from a couple towns over catch wind of the party and make quite an impression on your teammates. Legend of their beauty[74] makes its way to practice the following Monday. Turns out one of them is single. At the conclusion of track practice, you make your way to a computer faster than you can say "Jack Robinson."

Without regard for the availability of the family landline, you put on your detective cap to solve the mystery of how to find this gal on MySpace.[75] With a few keystrokes and clicks, you get a good look at them both and apply your teammates' standards onto the picture, immediately ranking their attractiveness and preferring one to the other. After conferring with your sources, you become mildly disappointed to find that your preferred girl isn't single. But just as she is whisked away, you convince yourself of her friend's pulchritude, ensuring that your opinion

73.   You can't be sure, but smart money says that you were already asleep or playing a one-player video game while this party was going on.

74.   Even during the infancy of social media, folks relied on verbal descriptions of people to ascertain their attractiveness. Or, as told by Hasan Minhaj in *Homecoming King*, you could just pursue a reputation without regard for looks.

75.   You actually remember trying to decide whether to commit to MySpace or Facebook. To this day, you will assert that MySpace was the more personalized, objectively better experience.

is consistent with prevailing peer beliefs. By the time you reach out to her, you've reassured yourself she's pretty hot. And according to your teammates, she is very friendly, a regular Miss Congeniality.

An online courtship as brief as a mayfly's life cycle yields positive results, and you prepare to visit her house for the first time[76] a mere week later. After selecting the optimal route, you realize that it will take you at least forty-five minutes for a one-way trip,[77] and you mentally tally up pre-emptive brownie points for making such a long trek. This belief is an inadvertent bastardization of the "Acts of Service" that you have seen demonstrated routinely by fictitious and actual male patriarchs as long as you can remember.

At their best, acts of service demonstrate to a loved one how much you care about them by donating time, being there in moments of crisis, and making them a priority in your life. In your pubescent understanding of AoS (for brevity's sake), they are mechanisms by which you can indebt a potential partner to you in exchange for romantic "feelings" in lieu of the ability to vulnerably express your own emotions out loud. Through no fault of their own, AoS may also be directly responsible for the infectiously catchy but cringeworthy "More Than Words" by one-hit wonder Extreme.

Such a long drive home gives you time to recount the events of the evening, and most are positive ones: sharing a first kiss, navigating parental authorities to orchestrate a stealthy finger bang, and feeling mildly exalted by her family and friends for being a niche kind of celebrity. Ms. Congeniality's dad in particular likes to pick your brain for nuggets of information on running training tips, shoe suggestions, and a scoop on the gossip regarding your competition. He makes you feel like you're the big man on campus, which you genuinely appreciate and wish your peers would share in his reverence.[78]

76. Remember trying to drive somewhere for the first time before your phone told you exactly where to go? The process involved something called MapQuest, and it was a hellscape.

77. The equivalent of 90-110 minutes today. AM, FM, cassettes and CDs were the only available automotive media at the time, thereby doubling the perceived time spent in a car.

78. He also shared with you one of the best family-friendly jokes you know: Q: What did the Pink Panther say when he stepped on an anthill? A: Dead ant, dead ant. Dead ant, dead ant, dead ant, dead ant ...

You approach this relationship with optimism and the diligence of a Ritalin-fueled undergraduate crossing items off her checklist. Dating, you calculate, ought to be governed by a catalog of yes/no questions you can ask yourself about any woman with whom you are in a relationship: Are you holding her hand? Check. Are you telling her she's pretty? Check. Are you talking for hours at a time on the phone? Check. Looks like you've got yourself a healthy relationship. One specific evening of box checking is seared into your memory, not so much for rousing conversation or intellectual discourse but for the lingering memory of something altogether different.

One evening together calls for a low-key hang-in, so you watch a movie through Comcast On Demand. You watch Johnny Knoxville's *The Ringer*—the cinematic masterpiece[79] where the protagonist pretends to have a disability so he can compete in the Special Olympics. Once the movie comes to a merciful conclusion, the On Demand menu pops up and plays on repeat as you two start fooling around. It's a song you find vaguely familiar, but can't quite place.

There you sit on the love seat, trying to discern whether that sound came from upstairs or the kitchen and who the soon-to-be accidental voyeur might be. What should you do with your hands on her chest? How hard is too hard to squeeze? Should you be involving more nipple? Is there an appropriate nipple-to-breast ratio of attention?

> *Bah bah, bah bah*[80]
> *This is the sound of settling*

How long should the boobs get attention? Is it time to take the grope train to the caboose?

> *Our youth is fleeting—*
> *Old age is just around the bend*

79. As clearly demonstrated by its 40 percent fresh rating on Rotten Tomatoes. Upon reflection, 40 percent was a generous rating.

80. You've often wondered who decides on the spelling of onomatopoeia. Is it the bands themselves? Is it the record label? The people who manually type out lyrics for karaoke establishments? And more importantly, you will disagree with the editor of this book on how many bah's are appropriate. The correct answer is four, no matter how much editorial services suggest three.

And I can't wait to go gray

How is this song still on? The movie ended literally an hour ago! The On Demand screen alerts you that the band playing is called Death Cab for Cutie. You opine that this is such a stupid name; they're trying way too hard to make a statement. And what's with this music video? It's just the band performing a series of random vignettes on a picture-within-a-picture-within-a-picture-within …

And I'll sit and wonder
Of every love that could've been
If I'd only thought of something charming to say[xi]

Accounting for the traffic, the distance, and the time of night, it should take about twenty-four "Sounds of Settling" before your unreasonably early weekend curfew, so you need to go. You leave simultaneously before you want to and long after you should have.

———

Weeks later, you offhandedly ask Ms. Congeniality if she wants to go to prom, less from desire and more from fear of the compulsory social stigma of not going to prom. You had not gone as a junior, publicly saying that you didn't want to spend the money but internally knowing you couldn't find a date. Feeling insufficient in this way sat with you and fermented for a year, causing you to ask your girlfriend before you otherwise would have. She dodges the question, and surprisingly, you don't freak out about it. After twenty minutes or so, she invites you to the sidewalk in front of her family's house, which had become a canvas for her chalk-based inquiry:[81] "Will you go to prom with me?"

A sense of moderate relief punctuates her romantic

81. This would be a highly Instagrammable moment today but is resigned to the Anecdotes and Memories file in the 2006 filing cabinet of your mind.

gesture—your future self would not be doomed to talking about your high school glory days as though you were cast into *Revenge of the Nerds*. Crisis averted. You give little regard to her artistry[82] but admit it was a sweet gesture. The interpersonal calculus you work out in your head suggests that your going to prom is only a logical consequence of being in a monogamous relationship at the end of your respective senior years.

As you leave for prom, Ms. Congeniality's dad hands you the keys to his car, a moderate upgrade from your silver 1992 Plymouth Voyager minivan nicknamed *Magnum*.[83] He instructs you to be careful with his baby—both of them. You don't realize how sitcommy this sounds in the moment, because that just seems like real life to you. On the ride over, your date's friend (the same one to whom you were initially attracted) compliments you, saying you're the most responsible guy she's ever been with. By this time last year, she had already passed out, drunk, and was being taken advantage of by her date. This revelation is rather shocking, but instead of feeling sorry for her, you pity yourself for having to go to prom with damaged goods, sloppy seconds. That's right, rather than feel badly for someone who had been date-raped, you focus on whether or not you want to deal with such heavy baggage in a relationship.[84] Using the yardstick of popular media, your prom is off to a very grim and decidedly non-magical start.[85]

You only know four people at this school, but on account of living up to her moniker, Ms. Congeniality is one of those popular, attractive girls who has many friends with whom to consort. Rather than go along, you remain at the table of strangers, feeling a bit like a discarded accessory.[86] The highlight of your night ends up being bonding with the folks at your assigned table over your mutual interest in the *Final Fantasy* video game series.[87]

The combination of feeling excluded, being relatively inept at engaging in unscripted social interaction, and trying to

82. For as much stock as you put into your own acts of service, you happen to struggle a bit with recognizing the investment when someone reciprocates an AoS to you.

83. As a tribute to the movie *Zoolander*, that is. No other connotations of this word played into choosing it as your car's nickname.

84. Social ineptitude be damned—your ability to contort any situation to feel like the victim yourself was actively reaching a toxic apex as you were perpendicular parking the car.

85. But it wasn't *Carrie* either. Funny how real life tends to fall under the thick part of a Gaussian distribution (or "bell curve" to the statistically uninitiated), but movies and music almost exclusively fall under the thin parts...

86. See also the scene in *Forgetting Sarah Marshall* where Peter holds Sarah's bags while she is being interviewed and photographed.

87. The stranger whose haunting pantomime of Tonberry King in a dimly lit high school cafeteria is an occasional recurring character in a few of your nightmares for the foreseeable future.

rationalize all the money you've spent on the evening starts your stomach churning. Your psychosomatic demons have come home to roost.

Reunited with your group, you all make for the limo, which takes you to an obscenely far away restaurant for dessert. Stomach still unsettled, you elect not to participate. The next stop is the tumbleweed of a town called Leroy. Your date has a connection who will sell alcohol to anyone, regardless of age, provided you are willing to pay the premium. But none for you, she mandates, because you are still in the midst of track season.

Rain has necessarily canceled your plans to camp outdoors, so the two of you set up the tent in the basement. Before tucking in, Ms. Congeniality's mother declares explicitly, "Good night," followed by a stern, "And no hanky-panky!" Thunder claps your rain cloud of a persona. You were hoping the evening might conclude with a storybook ending wherein you lost your virginity. Never mind that you were prophylactically ill-equipped or that your negativity all evening inevitably dampened the mood. You had held out hope until you heard those words. Instead, you cuddle up in the basement tent, and one of you sleeps very well. The other person is you.[88]

Rather than sleeping through the night, you more or less just remain awake until the alarm provides the sweet release of your captive arms and thereby your mobility. As a post-prom celebration, you all have to catch an early train to get to the baseball game on time. Here, you freeze your keister off, adding physical numbness to your figuratively numb emotional state. After your beloved Cubs get shut out, scraping together only three base runners, you sojourn home, concluding that this has been the worst weekend of your short life. You do not contact Ms. Congeniality for several weeks, and neither does she reach out to you. It was hardly the storybook ending promised by the silver screen.[89]

88. You will not be able to sleep comfortably next to another person until the second half of the Biden presidency. This was just your first taste of a sleepless embrace.

89. Only years later do you discover Kurt Vonnegut's opinion on the shape of stories, which rightfully critiques popular cinema and stories.

But the love-seeking junkie you are, you presume to have nowhere else to turn, so you run back to Ms. Congeniality a mere weeks later. The emptiness you feel appeals not to your reason and rationality but to that scary, emotive driver who is again at the wheel. In agreement, the two of you get back together during the summer months preceding your freshman year at different institutions of undergraduate learning. During this time, you still visit each other, commuting back and forth to each other's hometowns as often as you can afford to refill your gas tanks.

During one of the drives to her place, you get smacked in the face by a song called "Up in Arms" by your now-favorite band, Foo Fighters. Without pretext, context, or text of any other sort, you play it for her. It starts slowly, quietly, longingly:

> *It's true, the two of us*
> *Are back as one again*

Did she roll her eyes? Does she not get it? Dave Grohl and company lay it on pretty thick here. She has to understand why I picked the song for us. Maybe she does get it and just doesn't accept my feelings …

> *Together, now*
> *I don't know how*
> *This love could end*
> *My lonely heart,*
> *It falls apart*
> *For you to mend*[xii]

As your lime green iPod mini diminuendos to silence, you confirm with her that she did in fact understand your very obvious, surface-level reasoning for sharing the song. The combination of fear, anger, and not wanting to hear a negative reaction prevent you from engaging in a more meaningful conversation about your feelings, however. This was as vulnerable as you could be in the moment.

A week or so later, on a popular website dedicated to running, Ms. Congeniality poses a question: who is the most attractive high school male runner in the state? She offers many possible answers, at least two of whom are her former exes and one of whom is a friend. Your name does not make her list, imbuing you with a sense of betrayal. By your estimate, you've held up your end of the social contract by spending all your money on gas and all your free

90. Evidently, you expected her to be a mind reader because you don't recall explicitly telling her what you wanted out of fear that she wouldn't want to do or be those things.

91. This was untrue, of course, but was the first example you had ever experienced of *speed goggles*. You weren't famous but had made something of a name for yourself as an elite long-distance runner in your home state. You later realized that she was attracted to your status and not your stature. But at the time, you were glad anyone was attracted to anything about you at all.

92. Your cross country coach liked to describe this phenomenon as waking up in the morning and determining whether or not you should cut your arm off to get out of there. You know, once you got a good sober peak at her.

93. If you want to see the greatest birthday-themed episode of a television show, look no further than the season two episode of *Community*, titled "Mixology Certification." Happy Expulsion Day!

time on driving out to see her. You are acting out service and have become a little miffed that she's not reciprocating in a fashion consistent with your desires.[90] Living under the roof of the consummate 1950s couple allowed you to audit a class on the chemistry of marriage. In so doing, you learned the first law of Romantic Stoichiometry: any level of individual enjoyment must be counterbalanced with begrudging acquiescence to do a bunch of things you don't really want solely to demonstrate to her how much you care. In exchange, you expected her to barter in return with unconditional, monogamous affection. Instead, she gave you the nickname Boo-boo and allegedly was telling her friends that the two of you were fuck buddies.[91]

Despite this seemingly imbalanced equation, you deem Ms. Congeniality's transgression not egregious enough to make you want to ditch the security of having a long-distance relationship in your pocket as you embark upon the journey that will be your freshman year. In fact, you make her house the final stop en route to your new dormitory lodging.

———

At a time when your peers are all out meeting new people, many whose names they won't remember in the morning light,[92] you remain largely resigned to yourself, and a nightly phone call to the old ball and chain. You know, to keep checking that box.

Ms. Congeniality and two of your mutual friends plan a trip to come visit you on your birthday weekend, but a flat tire derails their plan. Instead of an in-person visit, you are serenaded by cell phone when the obligatory girlfriend phone call bleeds over from 11:59 p.m. into your actual birthday.[93] But truth be told, you aren't so sure that your better half would have remembered without the aid of her roommate and your mutual friend, who actually remembered.

So you spend your birthday, for the first time, as just another day at the proverbial office, since no one at school knows you very well yet. Apart from a few voicemails from family (obviously your twin brother) and two running friends from back home, this day manages to fly under the radar. On the bright side, Facebook now advertises your birthday to all your digital acquaintances, so wall posts serve as a proxy for sincere human interaction and annual well wishes.

Loneliness, on account of both your friends' inability to come visit and because this is the first time you have been away from family for so long, manifests itself as a slide into a psychological and emotional funk. Weeks later, when and MRI captures a tear in your right Achilles, that funk snowballs into clinically diagnosed depression. Making matters worse, the athletic trainer reveals that you likely tore the tendon months ago, but in your effort to secure a hero's ending[94] to your high school running career, the severity of the injury has probably worsened. Instead, you are forced to redshirt your freshman season to rehabilitate the injury while looking on from the sideline.

Furthermore, you have received your first-ever D on a test in general chemistry. Chemistry was much easier when you received partial credit on problems worked out by hand and graded by an instructor susceptible to mutual complaints about the state of the Cubs' bullpen. Dr. Isaacson has no such soft spot for you or any other nameless face in that lecture hall of 150 students.

And to top off all the uncertainty and tumult of being away from home for the first time, Ms. Congeniality has decided she wants to take a break. Without the proceeding "up," a break doesn't seem so bad, you try desperately to rationalize.[95] It's a temporary thing, you hope, but it doesn't stop the floodgates of your pessimism from opening. If only she hadn't gotten that damned flat tire …

94. While you had an outstanding track coach, he did employ a clichéd but effective tactic to inspire as much machismo as possible from your team by telling the story of how soldiers from Troy were most celebrated when they returned home lifeless, on their shields, as opposed to standing erect of their own volition.

95. Reminiscent of the Costanzian phonetic breakdown of the word "manure." Unfortunately for you and the women you date, your similarities to George Costanza do not end here.

Instead, you barrage a kind but unsuspecting girl from your calculus class with the details of your current relationship baggage. Between double-checking answers to your calc homework, she tries to comfort the sobbing mess you have become. The only things you knew about her before this admission were that she lived on the first floor of your dorm and that the two of you actually shared a birthday. It seemed like enough of a connection in your time of desperation.

The first weekend of your romantic break arrives, and thereby the first opportunity to get drunk free of social stigma. You, in competitive season, elect not to partake, but your recently-former -but-possibly-still-current girlfriend[96] wants to enjoy her college experience as fully as possible. Free from the burdens of social commitment, you tuck yourself into bed.

In the morning, you reflexively log on to AOL Instant Messenger,[97] discovering a litany of frantic messages from one of the friends who had planned to come visit for your birthday. This friend had clued you in on salacious behavior before, but this would be the last time. She divulges that your Ms. Congeniality cheated on you last night with some guy[98] at a track party.

A few hours later, your friend provides a relationship revelation: your modern-day Hester Prynne showed up to church with Arthur Dimmesdale, to the abject horror of your empathetic friend. There's no official word from your eyewitness as to whether they had changed clothes after spending the evening in each other's company. Your world has flipped on its axis, and the psychosomatic distress from prom night is back with a vengeance.

After a very tense couple of hours, you hear the contextually inappropriate tune of the Wham! smash hit, "Wake Me Up," which is accompanied by a strong vibration in your right pocket. She's finally calling. You summon the courage to pick up and face the music.

96. You, like Ross Gellar, were still foggy on the rules of a break.

97. In the minute before it is pronounced dead by the increasingly busy coroner of technology.

98. Some guy whose name you will still remember fourteen years after that fateful night - a name which will haunt you down the pasta aisle of the grocery store for years to come.

Speaking a bit timidly at first, Ms. Congeniality tells you, before you could get up the nerve to ask, about what happened the night before, corroborating your friend's account. No matter how many tearful reassurances and apologies are lofted your way, the pain just won't recede. Time passes in completely uneven intervals—moving first at a painstakingly glacial pace, eventually giving way to "Where did the past hour go?" speed. In total disbelief juxtaposed with seeming inevitability, you hang up the phone, crushed.

———

In a minor miracle, you make it through your obligations of the next two weeks. You are haunted by many thoughts, aspersions of her character and of your own worth, and the nagging emptiness that has consumed you in the past. You decide to call her up because you're not sure where else to turn, since you have overburdened your friend from calc class and she won't speak to you anymore. A different person with a different family dynamic may have called home instead. But you don't suspect June Cleaver and Mr. Father-Knows-Best are prepared to have a real conversation that can't be resolved in thirty minutes, including commercial breaks.

Still remembering Ms. Congeniality's number[99] despite deleting it from your phone, you dial her. She picks up, clearly glad to hear your voice. Walking to the uninhabited field on north campus in the calm of the night, you tell her you miss her. She reciprocates your sentiment. Is reconciliation possible? Is it worse to be alone or to mistrust your partner?

Defying all precedent in a rare display of self-worth, you end the phone call letting her know things are permanently over. The book is officially closed on this relationship, and you start

99. Still new to the world of cellular telephones, you had committed a few important digits to memory

trying to move on, with no idea of where to go, no map to help navigate, and a complete bankruptcy of emotional coping skills.

> *Bury me softly in this womb*
> *I give this part of me for you*

You tell yourself that your dating life will never be the same. You define yourself as a blameless victim in this series of events. Although you were on a break and she did nothing wrong by that mutually agreed-upon arrangement,[100] you continue to brand her with a scarlet letter both in your mind and to anyone who will listen to you speak on the subject.

> *Down in a hole and I don't know if I can be saved*
> *See my heart, I decorate it like a grave*

The synapses between your neurons responsible for trusting others have become a rocky chasm whose cliffs you won't be able to negotiate for quite some time.

> *You don't understand who they thought I was supposed to be*
> *Look at me now, a man who won't let himself be*

Moving forward, you find it cognitively easier for you to position her as the bad guy, so you can continue on your quest to live up to the prototype of the All-American, swell guy whom 1950s media trumpeted as worthy of aspiration.[101]

> *I'd like to fly*
> *But my wings have been so denied*[xiii]

100. So far as something like this can be mutual. Inevitably, one person wants a break, and the other does not. So what choice did you have?

101. While your wounds and scars may have matched exactly those of true domestic impropriety, you lacked the capacity to understand that you had inflicted them all upon yourself through this dichotomy of good and bad. When you showed others these scars, they sympathized with your overly simplistic logic, validating your simplified version of the truth, emboldening you to believe in your victimhood. As long as you adhere to these beliefs, you will experience recurring bouts of separation anxiety, an inability to trust wholly, and a crippling unwillingness to be vulnerable with those girls you try to court. Things do not start going well for you romantically for a very, very long while, hence the present publication.

3

WE WERE DEAD BEFORE THE SHIP EVEN SANK[xiv]

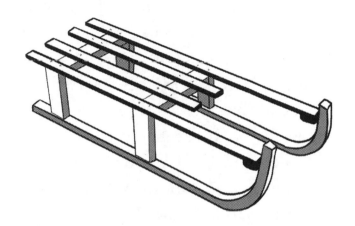

In the throes of this full-on depression, you turn to the last place you ever expected: therapy. After you complain to the athletic training staff about your onset insomnia, they encourage you to make an appointment with a therapist, skeptical though you are. Fortunately, a few visits to mental health experts are covered by university health insurance; otherwise you would never have spent your own money to go see someone proficient in the art of psychological quackery.[102]

But against all precedent, you attend your scheduled appointment, revealing the bare minimum about your feelings and experiences that have left you in such a state. One empathy-filled

102. Important backstory: your father once wondered aloud about depression treatment, "What are they going to do? Tickle my foot with a feather? Goochi, goochi, goo!" This hot take on mental health was met with knowing laughter from his brothers.

103. Your dad would only be more proud if you hadn't gone in the first place. But as it stands, you fell ass-backward into one of the healthiest practices of your entire life, even though you only met with this particular therapist once.

104. "Herm-udgeon" isn't wrong, but feels a little on the nose.

hour later, you exit the facility, oscillating between feeling relief and being embarrassed that you couldn't figure this all out on your own. You do not return for subsequent counsel because if therapy really works, one session ought to be enough to help, if not cure you altogether, right?[103]

In the wake of having been "cheated on," you remain involuntarily single and celibate for a few more years. Mounting insecurities bubble up into your conscious mind, and you find the thought of facing them head-on, let alone letting a romantic partner know they exist, to be a wellspring of anxiety. In your Sport Psychology class, you learn that the motivation to achieve success eclipses the motivation to avoid failure.[xv]

With respect to dating and socializing in general, you fall somewhere along the spectrum between hermit and curmudgeon,[104] not even feigning interest in being sociable. Given that you have identified the precipitating factor in your most recent breakup to be alcohol, you abstain from the stuff completely, which hardly endears you to campus life in a college town surrounded by cornfields. When you do feel socially obligated to attend parties thrown by your teammates, this abstinence coupled with your sardonic persona guarantees that your presence in a room will empty it within five minutes … like clockwork. You add this to the confirmation of your perceived victimhood, leading you to wonder why you left home in the first place.

Speaking of home, the fall semester of your junior year is coming to a close. Procrastinating from studying for finals and longing for home, you inadvertently log in to the newly unveiled Facebook Messenger. An old friend (one of the two who called you on your birthday two years ago) from your high school days is online, so you decide to chat her up and see what she's doing for the holidays. You met her at an All-Star cross country meet your senior year and have kept in periodic contact since then. At the time, she was seeing someone, spoken for, taken. But this seems to no longer be the case, as Ms. Taken suggests the two of you plan a "date" during your winter vacation, a proposition to which you excitedly agree.[105]

In the two days separating you from Christmas break, your mood improves perceptibly. Rather than harboring contempt for the smug frat boys[106] walking with their glamorous girlfriends in tow, you grant them the universal head nod, wordlessly conveying "Nice work, bro." Your internal dialogue has shifted from an envious zero sum game to a hope that you are about to join the exclusive fraternity of coupled life. No longer is the bro your foe and rival suitor, but just some dude in hot pursuit of a physical relationship. This entire mindset changed for you literally overnight, just at the prospect of a date.

You decide to meet up at a sort of midway point between your house and hers, then carpool the rest of the way, lest you spoil the surprise of the location and activity. Ms. Taken's sister will later call you a scholar and a gentleman, titles you have only earned on behalf of your gender setting a criminally low bar. A true gentleman might have just picked her up, but you weren't sure you'd have enough money for gas that week if you'd made the whole trip.

One of the best Christmas light displays in your hometown occupied the same land as your old high school's cross country course—a romantic little nod to how the two of you had met. After you pass the seals juggling Santa's presents,[107] you produce two sleds from the suspiciously large trunk[108] of your car. This first date—sledding at a cross country course with Christmas lights—had been carefully planned to extract sentiment and nostalgia with the express intent to make her swoon and faint

105.   Time will reveal she meant this colloquially, but your literally-interpreting brain and famished heart concoct a different interpretation altogether.

106.   Of whom there were many. Imagine every possible permutation of Paul Ryan and Ben Roethlisberger making up the entire male student body.

107.   Better known as the 5K start line from August through October.

108.   Seriously, were the mid-2000s Chevy Impalas designed by bootleggers?

like the idyllic prototype of femininity that may have been popular in the 1920s.

Your mental elbow grease pays off, and by the time you return to her car, she seems to have also changed the meaning of *date* in her mind to one more closely resembling the nonplatonic definition on which you had based the evening. There is an unspoken agreement to declare a thumb war between your tongues.

This having been just the second night of Christmas break, you are bound and determined to see her several more times before the spring semester pries the two of you away from your neighboring hometowns. You bail on family and friends, instead opting to join her for a few days and nights at school before you journey across time zones to your own campus. The one-hour time difference in her favor makes it difficult for you to remain awake during your newly-scheduled nightly conversations.

———————

Looks like we made it—
Look how far we've come, my baby
We mighta took the long way
We knew we'd get there someday

Fairly early into dating, you buy Ms. Taken a shirt from a company specializing in snarky graphic T-shirts, which reads "Long Distance Relationship" and features clip art runners executing a baton handoff. Congratulations are in order, you believe, for orchestrating such a clever, witty, and semi-subtle marking of your territory from four hundred miles away while also appearing to be a generous boyfriend.

The two of you grow to enjoy the challenge of staying together in the face of the perilous pitfalls[109] plaguing those engaged in long-distance relationships.

109.   Your inside joke became calculating the percentage of days you had even seen each other while you were dating. You have never professed and will never profess to be good at flirting...

Ain't nothing better[110]
We beat the odds together
I'm glad we didn't listen—
Look at what we would be missing[xvi]

On the good days, it feels like fighting the proverbial good fight and defeating the infantry of "The Odds" in their bitterly waged war against Romance. You fancy yourself the white knight, calling on every walk to and from class, staying up late to take her incoming calls, and driving home as often as possible to see her. Once, you even miss a track meet, telling your coach you are *going home,* just to squeeze in an extra weekend together. You explain to her that you hadn't lied to your coach on the technicality that "home is where the heart is." Each time you visit her in the frigid hellscape of the upper Midwest, you skip classes and practice on Friday and/or Monday to make the trip feel more financially worthwhile. By every metric you know to calculate, you are totally committed to the relationship.

Once the fall semester wraps up, you have secured a summer job in Ohio, marking the first time you will spend non-school months away from home. When you share the good news with her, she explains that she isn't sure the relationship will last because it was too hard not seeing you during the school year. After a brief discussion, she plainly states that if you plan to work out of state over the summer, she will end things. To save the relationship, you quit the job and move home the following day.[111]

Later in the summer, long after quitting your job to move back home to make things work with Ms. Taken, you take a road trip with your brothers: a cross-country journey to cross off the baseball parks in Pittsburgh and Washington, DC.[112] During this time, she leaves you a voicemail, but inexplicably, you demonstrate uncharacteristic fortitude, refraining from listening to the message while on your trip. This turns out to be a trip-saving endeavor.

110. While Shania Twain rocks the original, the Akie Bermiss-led Lake Street Dive cover is otherworldly. Hearing that cover in person will be one of your greatest concert memories of all time.

111. Years later, you would learn in an unpolished but informative eulogy that one of your uncles had dropped out of college, forsaking his basketball scholarship, to drive back home the very night he heard another guy had half the mind to get sweet on his high school sweetheart.

112. Just to be clear, the trip was primarily designed to see fireworks and baseball games, not anything of cultural significance—a major regret of yours to this day.

When you finally return home, you listen to the message. In it, she explains that she had been out drinking and skinny-dipping with a group of friends, her ex-boyfriend included. Thinking back on it, you are quite sure you would have ruined your phone on account of throwing it straight into the Reflecting Pool. But instead of ruining the trip and causing a scene at the Lincoln Memorial, her admission only ruins the following evening. With intractable anger, betrayal, and sadness, you walk out of your parents' house barefoot on a humid summer night to return Ms. Taken's call.

She never lets me in
Only tells me where she's been
When she's had too much to drink

By this point, your disdain for alcohol has been extremely well documented. She is also intimately aware of your jealousy-fueled disdain for her ex, even though she has assured you that your insecurities are unfounded.

I just run my hands through her dark hair
Then I pray to God, "You gotta help me fly away"[113]

113.   This is definitely your least pleasant memory associated with Hootie and the Blowfish. Your most fond recollection is the time your grandpa referred to the band as "Hobo and the Blowholes." Looking back, you're sure his mispronunciation was for comedic effect and you dearly miss his sense of humor.

Why the hell is *she* crying? You are the victim here—minding your own damn business, taking a single weekend off from seeing her to do something with your family, and this is how you get treated?

It is well past your bedtime, but you are still pacing around outside so you don't wake anyone up with this conversation. You have circled back to the same conversation points a dozen times now. She's Muhammad Ali on the ropes, and you are an increasingly exhausted George Foreman.

Let her walk right out on me
And if the sun comes up tomorrow
Just let her be[xvii]

Even though you know it's time to break up, the sorrow and remorse in her pleading voice convince you otherwise. On the other end of the line, she wonders tearfully, "You're not going to break up with me now, are you?" Prior to finding her as your personal romantic oasis, you had spent nearly two years crossing a desert of desperate loneliness, and the very thought of making that journey again puts sand in all the unpleasant nooks and crannies of your brain. Instead, you agree to share a drink called loneliness, which, as Billy Joel will tell you, is better than drinking alone.

————

After the requisite four years, you have earned your bachelor's degree and feel entitled to a job. The epicenter of your entire job search is Ms. Taken. She is taking a fifth year to graduate because not only is chemistry hard, but she also has another year of athletic eligibility left.[114] Due in part to such a geographically limited search radius, you have about as many job prospects as a fireworks store has customers on November 17. Out of financial practicality, you move back in with your folks and little brother, but you are also closer to the girl. Come to think of it, switch the order of those statements.

You end up working three part-time jobs to pay off what's left of your student loans. The benefit of such an economic setup is that, for three months of your salary, you could afford to feed the quarter machine at the Kmart uptown until you found the prettiest ring.[115] Your precontemplation of searching in earnest for rings may have less to do with your actual feelings and more to do with the fact that after dating for two years, it seems like it's time to start thinking this way.

About a month after the fall semester begins, you plan to drive up and see Ms. Taken, intending to make the trip with

114.   In a gut-wrenching story for another time, you also had eligibility left but did not use it due to a badly broken ankle.

115.   Just a few months prior, you had found the printed receipt of the ring your twin brother bought for his then-fiancée, now wife. That was an awkward verbal exchange.

a friend who has professional business up in her neck of the woods. If not for your 3:1 work-to-life-balance ratio, you may even have gotten to make the trip to hang out with them both. Instead, you crash your car on the way to your first-ever cross country practice as a coach.

———

It is quite a scene—the fire department, state police, county police, and squad cars from three municipalities all converge at this intersection. Turns out it has been rated the deadliest crossroads in the entire county. But thankfully, this crash does not bolster this statistic, and no one is really even hurt, although the official report indicates that the officer of the cop car into which you crashed was "incapacitated,"[116] which is the biggest hyperbole in the entire history of the known universe.

You feel fine physically, but your car and pride are both totaled because the accident happened literally sixty feet from the cross country course, and your athletes could see you as they ran by. The head coach was out of town for the weekend and had left you in charge of running the show. He was more of a sprints guy, anyway, so you were really excited for the chance to handle the distance crew on your own.

Because no one was hurt, the worst parts of the evening are (1) knowing your car insurance premium will increase and (2) telling Ms. Taken that you won't be able to visit for the weekend. Incidentally, the crash had taken place in front of the very same park where the two of you shared a night sledding on your first date.[117]

The sun rises, the earth spins, and her weekend goes on much the same as it would had you been there. In an attempt to make it up to your girlfriend for not being up there, you try sneaking in a few extra calls. Uncharacteristically, she is unable to answer, so

116.   A whole separate book could be dedicated to telling the ins and outs of this accident and what it demonstrated about racism among the police departments of the area, the validity of eyewitness testimony, the truth-obscuring of law enforcement, the integrity of small-town news media, and the seeds for the fallout of your relationship with your father—but all that is beyond the scope of this book.

117.   Were this a fiction novel or film, the car crash scene in front of the location of your first date while speaking to her on the phone would be justifiably labeled "a little too on-the-nose" foreshadowing. But as a memoir, you just have to believe it.

you (rightly) assume she has gone out to drink with her friends. She has called you while buzzed enough times, and you have expressed your disapproval enough times for both of you to know it is best to avoid this type of communication altogether. Blissful ignorance is the agreed-upon policy, and for its part, it works well enough. In fact, you use this information to rationalize that it is actually good you aren't visiting because it means you don't have to be around all the drinking. Your absence makes you, and thereby your company, all slightly less miserable.

In lieu of the extra calls and conversations, you decide to expand upon your cursory search for engagement rings, in part to make up for not being able to visit and, again, because the timing seems about right.[118] Plus, you now have the time to peruse, since you don't have to spend it all battling traffic and pretending to be friendly and happy while at a brewery. You shudder at the prospect and take solace in knowing you have averted a crisis.

118. As much as you admire, respect, and love your twin brother, he once said the second most offensive thing you have ever heard. When asked if he was excited to get married, he said, "I'm excited that it's the next logical step in our relationship." Somewhere, a Vulcan just blew a load.

A drama-free week rolls by, which is just what you need after the municipal circus of last Friday. Your car is in the shop, getting fixed, and none of your athletes give you too much grief. Considering that most of them are only two to four years younger than you, this is quite a victory. A sense of relief actually rolls over you. You feel as though you have just found the bottom of the pool with your feet after a serious struggle and gasping for air. You happily await the late-night call from Ms. Taken, facetiously enjoying videos of Jim Rome dissecting sports to help pass the time.

You put the boom into my heart
You send my soul sky high when your lovin' starts
Jitterbug into my brain
Goes a bang-bang-bang 'til my feet do the same

119. You enjoyed this song because of its exceptional use to comedic effect in the movie *Zoolander,* not for its own merits or out of true appreciation for the genius of George Michael, which you would later possess.

Your phone has a remarkably high-fidelity Wham! ring-tone,[119] at least by 2011 telephonic standards. The chipper tone in your voice matches the joy of the song.

Something ain't right
My best friend told me what you did last night
Left me sleepin' in my bed
I was dreamin' but I should've been with you instead[xviii]

After a quick greeting, she confides that she just guilt-ate an entire box of Cheez-Its, and you need to have the "we need to talk" talk. Considering you were literally just looking at engagement rings in your non-Jim-Rome browser, this seemingly out-of-nowhere topic catches you badly off guard. She confides the stress-induced cheesy carbohydrate binge to you in what feels like an attempt to elicit sympathy and/or empathy, evidently forgetting to whom she is speaking.

Of course there's another guy. How else would you explain this? Ms. Taken freely admits that you have done nothing wrong. You belabor the question several times over, her answer affording you the sense of moral righteousness. You now basically throw your hands into the air and back away like you're trying to convince a referee of your innocence in not committing a foul. This psycho-emotional absolution plays a key role in the narrative you spin about how you're always the victim, and she's just given you golden yarn.

She doesn't say who he is though. Or who she is. It's the 2010s, and you're starting to realize that sexuality exists on a spectrum. Two of your previous girlfriends have made explicit mention of wanting to be with another girl. Your pseudoconservative Christian upbringing lays out the blueprint for your brain to process the thought of same-sex couples the same way a laminator would process a salamander. Other aspects of your anatomy adopt a far more progressive view. Maybe someone finally responded to the Craigslist personal ad she posted before the two of you started dating. Who knows?

You sulk to yourself, the cloaked specter of depression beckoning.

———

Days turn into weeks as every minute seems like an hour. While your parents are more than willing to continue housing and feeding you free of charge, you feel the impulse to leave as soon as is feasible. The entire college track team you're coaching gets busted and subsequently arrested for underage drinking at a party they've hosted the night before their final indoor meet. One of them posts a Facebook status update from the back of the squad car around one o'clock in the morning. Clearly, you reason, there is nothing left for you here.

So you start applying to graduate schools because that's what happens in times of stunted economies. You aren't meeting any new people in the basement of your parents' house—and not many folks in your hometown of 13,000. In this time of desperation, a neurotransmitter fires a message never before housed in your brain: what if I start drinking? Is it time to start doing as the Romans are doing? If I move far enough away, no one in my family will ever even have to know about it.

You start doing the mental legwork to determine which schools and programs are even still accepting applications. The growing disdain you harbor for cold weather precludes your search from going anywhere north. Suddenly, advertisements to visit Tennessee, Kentucky, and Missouri start to populate the ad spaces on webpages you visit. Amid all the research, you treat yourself to a social media break.

Somehow, you have been logged out of your Facebook account, and it directs you to the login page.[120] As you click to log

120. Critique and complain away about a world overrun by apps, but not having to sign into a service every GD time is the most convenient aspect of life in the twenty-first century.

in, you realize there are autofill options apart from your own email address. Morbidly curious, you see what other profiles are at your fingertips. First a moment of abject terror hits you, followed by a moral dilemma—Ms. Taken left her login and password saved to your computer.

You should obviously delete it. Clearly, it would be wrong to invade someone's privacy like this. To proceed any further would be a violation of trust, a breach in the social contract among the citizenry. WWJD? The golden rule creeps int—

You're in with one click. Hell hath no fury like a heartbroken millennial with access to another person's social media account. You feel the shame and disappointment of Jiminy Cricket, having sold out on your conscience so quickly.

Within the first ten seconds, you know whodunnit, solving the riddle of who turned Ms. Taken into Ms. Taken Away. The secret identity of the thief[121] is none other than the Wilco-loving, job-having, gremlin-postured runner in your social circle… the friend you were supposed to ride up with to see her before your car crash. The broken pieces of your heart shatter again. This motherfucker has met your family. You saw him at a cross country meet literally the weekend after he got back from visiting her. How. Could. He?

Gluttonously, you seek out just a little more punishment.

Looks like they have a conversation thread going back and forth, and it is filled with hallmark words and phrases of the honeymoon phase of a relationship. Exclamation points, smiley emoticons, and worst of all, song lyrics:

> First there's rules about old goats like me
> Hanging 'round with chicks like you
> But I do like you
> And another one—
> You say "like" too much

121. A decade passes before you realize there is no thief, but instead that the two of you were horrible together in every conceivable way, but too insecure to leave one another.

Every emotion in your 8-bit catalog comes out, full force and in simultaneity.[122] Admiration of similar music was the actual start to your relationship. The very first time the two of you first met, you carpooled to a cross country meet together and listened to Dynamite Hack's cover of Eazy E's "Boyz n the Hood,"[123] each with one earbud. This was too much, man.

> *But I'm shaking at your touch*
> *I like you way too much*
> *My baby, I'm afraid I'm falling for you*[124] xix

A gentle blue light emitted from your computer screen and the hum of your CPU filled the otherwise dead still and silent air of your parents' basement. Dumbly, you occupied the intersection of a Venn Diagram plotting "Betrayed," "Bewildered," "Gobsmacked," and "Lost"

122. Do you ever have those moments when you realize there must be some other form of a common word? Like, people are overwhelmed or underwhelmed all the time, but no one talks about being whelmed. If a day is said to be dreary, shouldn't the word *drear* be a noun that we use almost as much of the time? Usage of the English language is fascinating.

123. It took you far too long to realize there was an original before the Dynamite Hack cover. Once you were aware, the line about "her nappy-ass weave" made a lot more sense.

124. And they did fall for each other. Years later, they were wed in holy matrimony, but not before you wasted countless hours tormenting yourself with thoughts of what could have been, feeling betrayed, deleting pictures, donating clothes of yours that she liked, throwing away gifts she gave you, hitting the next button on your iPod mini when "Motorcycle Drive By" came on shuffle, trying to forget her phone number after she begged you to commit it to memory, and painfully recalling her specific routine for making peanut butter and jelly sandwiches. It would be years before you could listen to *Pinkerton* again without a handful of tissues to soak up the tears you didn't feel like men were supposed to cry.

4
TELL ME I'M PRETTY[xx]

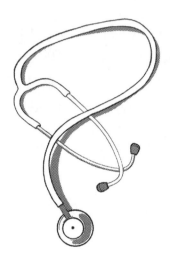

It's a jump to the left
And a step to the right
With your hands on your hips
You bring your knees in tight
But it's the pelvic thrust
That really drives you insane
Let's do the time warp again![xxi]

You are quite uncertain what, exactly, is even happening around you. Your typically mild-mannered girlfriend just rushed the stage with a single dollar bill in her cleavage, and a man involved in this production plucked it from her bra with the fluidity of a pelican snatching its marine breakfast. Audience members are singing secret lyrics and blurting out calls and responses synchronized to windshield wipers, among a thousand other oddities per minute. In some ways, you know less about *Rocky Horror Picture Show* now than before the show started.[125] Any way you size it up, this is hardly the dullest Halloween evening you spend in graduate school.

——————

Around this time, you start straightening the bearings of your independence. Having secured a teaching assistantship, you have entered the world of paying your own bills—on a meager $7,000 per year salary, booned by a side hustle finding the right color and size shoes for mall patrons. Paradise it isn't, but you are starting to enjoy this feeling of being self-made.

For the first time, you successfully utilize the platform of online dating, although it manifests itself in friendship. You strike up a digital conversation with a fellow graduate student from another department, and she invites you to a soiree with her colleagues. Unsure whether she is networking or vetting you as a potential partner (but also too afraid to ask for clarification), you go hang out with her crew. Immediately upon entering the apartment, you get the feeling that you are deeply entrenched in the friend zone with the girl you had hoped to pursue romantically. She introduces you as a friend to her other friends, who in turn introduce you to their friends.[126] One of these ancillary acquaintances had also met Ms. Friend Zone through the same dating site you used. In the past, the fight-or-flight reaction of your sympathetic nervous system would have dictated your next moves. But rather than locking horns and competing for her affection, you and this other suitor strike up an easy conversation, and by the end of the night you consider him a friend.

Though not entirely sure she thinks of you in the same way, you think Ms. Friend Zone the smartest,[127] most attractive

125.   *Rocky Horror* will become one of your most treasured memories of all time, though not on the merits of the performance on this night. Years later, your mom will tell you that she and her friend took your dad and his brother on a double date to see *RHPS*, which you find to be uproariously funny given that your paternal family is so straightlaced, conservative, and quick to vilify anything that falls outside their margins of acceptable.

126.   See also: fundamental pillar of pyramid schemes.

127.   She once texted you a message that included the phrase "cómo se dice 'wasteyface'?" causing you to nearly pop a button off your trousers.

woman you would ever be able to date. Like driftwood in the tide, the sharp, jagged edges of your negative feelings toward alcohol consumption have worn down and smoothed out. This comes in handy as you hang out with her cohort each week in the hopes that you can shift this relationship from reverse into a forward-traveling gear. In the meantime, your laser focus has shifted slightly from the potential romance with Ms. Friend Zone to enjoying the already-palpable friendships you have forged with mutual friends. To be sure, elation would envelop you if she agreed to date, but her friends—whom you initially considered to be an afterthought— are becoming an increasingly delightful bunch.

As such, you do your best to try and play it cool and slow with Ms. Friend Zone. You help her whitewash some furniture she picked up while thrifting. You help her dog sit, despite your wariness of dogs, and you accompany her to church one Sunday, despite your wariness of gods. You really like her, and your willingness to try these other things to be close to her conveys that pretty obviously in your mind, but you're still not so sure where she stands.

You confide in a friend from undergrad how much you like Ms. Friend Zone and periodically bother her for advice about what to say to your crush. One response is a link to a song from Disney's *The Little Mermaid*:

> *My, oh, my*
> *Look at the boy too shy,*
> *He ain't gonna kiss the girl*[128]
> *Sha-la-la-la-la-la*
> *Ain't that sad,*
> *Ain't it a shame, too bad,*
> *He gonna miss the girl* [xxii]

128. Over the years, you have been burnt with bad advice from singing crabs (who hasn't?), but Sebastian was right on the money, for once.

The song and your college friend are both right—you know this. But you have an express inability to take the chance of being wrong, of imposing your wishes upon her[129]—this much is immediately apparent to you. What will take much longer to realize is that you are, and have always been, terrified of rejection and getting hurt. The pain of previous relationships still dictates your decisions, leaving you emotionally ill-equipped to face the very real possibility that she, or the next girl you try to date, may not reciprocate your feelings.

One night, you muster up the courage to threaten to kiss her if she gets any closer. It's a move that, if deployed on your second or third encounter, may have conveyed the smooth confidence of which you clearly have none. But considering it has been at least six weeks since she began subtly expressing interest in you, this maneuver at best elicits in her a sense of relief. Luckily for you, she possesses saint-like patience.

After the seal has been broken, the two of you are attached at the lips. In fact, you spend the following evening at a Halloween party[130] mostly disengaged from socializing, instead favoring a spirited match of tonsil hockey, which goes into double over-time. Between bouts of tongue lashing, she manages to sneak in half a dozen Jell-O shots, while you largely abstain from alcohol consumption, much to the consternation of your peers. In their drunkenness, this concern is based on peer pressure and a groupthink mindset. But in their sobriety, they fairly question the morality of your actions and intent. That's okay; your will is good, you assure them.

As the evening winds to a close, you lay down the law[131] and persuade Ms. Friend Zone to turn in for the evening. Because she is dogsitting, you accompany her to the domicile of her canine-owning boss. As her current brain chemistry is riddled with alcohol molecules, she insists the two of you sleep in the

129. Having been kissed unsuspectingly, yourself, in kindergarten.

130. In retrospect, you suspect that you were at the same party as one of your future therapists, though you never explicitly confirm this with her.

131. You were dressed as a cowboy. Guess that's an important visual for this wordplay to work.

132. A few weeks later, you will peddle some mall shoes and apparel to the gentleman in whose bed you have slept, providing a nice moment of intrigue to an otherwise mind-numbingly boring day working retail with nearly competent coworkers.

133. It is at this point that you have iceboxed her so hard that she could have nicknamed her genitalia "Ms. Freeze."

134. Seriously—watch this movie. You'll enjoy this present work way more if you just watch it already. This is why bookmarks were invented.

primary bedroom rather than the guest space to which she ordinarily sleeps.[132] This, of course, takes place after you have chased and miraculously captured the two escaped dogs. Perhaps inebriated late-night dog catching was the skill which had earned your date the job in the first place,

That night, all the two of you do is sleep,[133] and the same goes for the next morning and the subsequent weekend at her place. Because your immediately preceding relationship had moved too quickly, you have very badly overcorrected in this relationship. Her needs woefully unmet, she sends you a text the following day to let you know that things aren't working out. A mature, well-adjusted adult may have asked for clarification and to talk in person, but you decide, instead, to spend your afternoon getting hammered and watching the incomparably funny *Forgetting Sarah Marshall*[134] while continuing to miscommunicate via text with Ms. Friend Zone.

A mutual friend lets you know that she actually just wanted more physical affection from you and didn't mean to communicate that the two of you were through. But in your now-predictable pattern of catastrophic thinking, you slammed the brake through the floor of the car, a la Fred Flintstone. Again, you have fashioned yourself into the victim as you recount the story to your friends, hoping exclusively for their sycophancy during your time of vulnerability. In a new development, your sophomoric interpersonal aptitude extends not only to the relationship but also to mutual friends. Who says you can't teach an old dog new tricks?

With time and a few hyperbolic circumstances, you become sworn enemies with the woman you had recently adored. In an altercation between Ms. Friend Zone and one of her friends, you take the side of the friend. In accordance with your allegiance, Ms. Ex-Friend Zone requests you never speak to each again, and you dutifully oblige.[135] The peer group gets divided up as in a custody battle, and some of her colleagues are yours to keep with full visitation rights. Many others are unlikely to ever see you again.

Of the friends you retain, two decide to take you to the *Rocky Horror Picture Show* at midnight one evening….

———

A few weeks before you met Ms. Transylvania for *Rocky Horror*, she had gotten dumped by a friend of yours. Considering the two of you had barely spoken ten words to one another, you felt surprised when she asked to meet up for that midnight showing. In any case, you decide to be a supportive friend, accompany her to the show, and watch her feed a man on stage a dollar bill from her bosom.

And for a good long while, you are able to remain this role as a platonic support giver to this new friend of yours. She has openly wept in front of you, and seems completely crestfallen, turning to you out of desperation and a crippling loneliness that you happen to recognize. But when the levee of feelings breaks, her emotions spill out into a text explaining how she has become romantically interested in you. The void created by your last breakup, now nearly a year ago, coupled with a deep, intimate understanding and empathy for how she feels, results in the perfect storm of motives for you to start seeing her.

A few dates hence, you are hyper awkward. Imagine Judd Apatow directing Sheldon from *The Big Bang Theory* level of awkward. Ms. Transylvania evidently doesn't notice or mind and asks you point-blank one night:

"Do you want to have sex with me?"[136]

135. A few months later, you see her on campus, elude her by turning down a sidewalk you don't normally take, and end up late to a meeting because you get lost.

136. Admittedly, this work is subject to the same paradigms of memory as a function of time and cannot be one hundred percent accurate. But, as indicated by the sanctity of the quotation marks, this line is presented verbatim, seared into your permanent memory bank. Who says "with me"? Isn't that implied?

As you've gotten older, this is the exact level of candor[137] you require to engage in any act of romance for the first time. So even though you had not intended for her to be the second woman with whom you have ever slept, she takes what the cool fundamentalist Christian kids call your "secondary virginity" that night.[138]

─────────

Because of the vulnerable nature of this relationship, your role as the consoler thrives. In the words of the Dread Pirate Roberts, "It was the *please* that caught[xxiii]" your memory. You suspect, or at least rationalize, that sleeping with Ms. Transylvania will make her feel better, more confident, and thereby healthier for future relationships. After all, is there any truer act of service than making someone feel sexually viable? And would it be the worst thing in the world if, incidentally, you also benefited from the arrangement? In about two months, you are scheduled to pursue a terminal degree three time zones away, and this will be the expiration date of any romantic entanglement with this nice, very intelligent doctoral student.

You are generally not one to kiss and tell,[139] but matters in the bedroom are not up to your standard. Somehow, the sex in this relationship is worse than not having sex in the previous one. Due to the inherent life cycle of this relationship, you have envisioned (but failed to articulate) that this would be a fun and casual fling. It turns out to be monotonous and unenjoyable, bordering on burdensome. In fact, you lament about it to a friend, likening the relationship to playing tennis with a spent ball, having lost its bounce entirely. Sure, you can still play, but you really have to work and whack the hell out of the ball, and your shoulder is getting exhausted.[140] But had you communicated these feelings to her at the time, the two of you could

137. The most glaring example of your obliviousness came when a woman wearing a Batman shirt told you she had matching underwear, and you failed to catch her subtext. Evidently you were waiting for the bat signal.

138. She would also be the sixth woman with whom you ever slept, taking what the *really* cool fundamentalist Christian kids call your "senary virginity" some time later.

139. Present publication notwithstanding.

140. Hardly the description you expected of the very same woman who rushed the stage brassiere-first at the *Rocky Horror Picture Show*. But life is full of interesting juxtapositions like this.

have discussed your next steps together and chosen to either work on improving things or going separate ways.[141]

Matriculation leads to the inevitable conclusion of this romance. Whereas you will continue your studies on the Pacific Coast, Ms. Transylvania's own studies will keep her tethered to west Appalachia, and you have precisely the amount of sense required to not attempt a long-distance relationship with her. After some convincing, she agrees to an exclusively platonic arrangement, on the condition that you don't tell her if/when you start dating someone new.

The second care package she sends you coincidentally arrives the same day as your second date with a girl from the Valley (but the antithesis of a Valley Girl). At this point, you feel compelled to break your pact with Ms. Transylvania. She very clearly has a sense of hope in a future for the two of you. The ensuing phone conversation goes about as well as you would expect.

———————

Three time zones away from anywhere you've ever called home, you jockey for purchase in hopes of securing a footing in a PhD program. Having been explicitly courted by your adviser, you are convinced to put your chips all-in on yourself. Anxiety and crippling self-doubt be damned—you're going to earn a doctorate! You are already the first (just a few days ahead of your twin brother) to receive a bachelor's degree, the first to hold a master's degree, and now the first to live outside of the Midwest (hold your late aunt who had lived in Washington state about a decade ago).

A month after your arrival into the Pacific Time Zone, your twin brother becomes a father to a beautiful baby boy. Your grandmother has a stroke just a few weeks after that. These are the reasons you ultimately cite to your adviser in the case to discontinue your studies, but the truth is even simpler and more juvenile: you

141. This did not happen, and you are writing a book about this lesson left painfully unlearned. And you suspect that her book would describe you in deservedly less than glowing terms.

feel mentally inadequate among a group of such bright folks, and that really smart, cute Valley girl, totally, like, dumped you.

The first aforementioned claim is easily and succinctly described. Everyone in your program is your intellectual superior, has real-life experience in the field of higher education, and maintains a clear sense of their objectives in the program. You don't. At the heart of your departure, though, is another relationship gone south, which leads you to overreact, panic, and leave. In other words, play #2 from your Breakup Playbook.[142]

This is the first time you actually like someone so much it wracks your nerves to the point of timidity. While preparing for your first date, you frantically switch in and out of every conceivable permutation of nice clothes you own, before eventually picking one. After dinner concludes, you get lost on your drive back home because you couldn't stop thinking about Dr. Valley Girl and what it meant when she hugged but did not kiss you at night's end.

This Valley Girl is going to school to be a real doctor.[143] She's funny, she's beautiful, and—as you have become wont to say—she's the most attractive woman you could plausibly date. She is interested in the research you have done and plan to do. She has an attachment to a rivaling undergraduate institution from the Midwest. Your only suspicion is to wonder why, despite all of these great qualities and topics of conversation, she likes the likes of you. Bewildering. Things go well until, of course, they don't.

Strict adherence to grammar is an early point of shared snobbery. Your mutual affinity for grammatical sanctity causes her to lend you her copy of *Eats, Shoots & Leaves*[xxiv] which delights your sensibilities. She's vegetarian, which apparently is a whole thing out here on the West Coast, and you try your darndest to accommodate. Luckily, you discover the French fry loophole, which defines any self-respecting vegetarian. In fact, you studied up on the whole vegetarian topic prior to your first date[144] and

142. Bluff called. Like Vince Vaughn's character in *Wedding Crashers*, you don't actually have other plays in your book.

143. A self-effacingly important distinction regularly made among doctors of philosophy in varying disciplines.

144. Yes—another online date. It seemed like a crutch at the time, but the way the dating scene changed with websites and apps had not yet erased the stigma in your 24 year old mind.

thought you dazzled her with your uniquely clever inquiry: "So why are you a vegetarian?"

In your magnum opus to accommodating her dietary needs, you prepare a Valentine's Day dinner. Never mind that you had not planned far enough in advance to make reservations at a nice place; this is about demonstrating your affection through loving and considerate acts. The entrée is not worthy of earning you Michelin Star status, but you stand by the chocolate-covered strawberries for dessert. You also stand by Dr. Valley Girl's prescription that this night needs a spirited game of Super Mario World, whereby a stage clear or a death means losing an article of clothing.[145] It is at this moment that you fearfully decide you cannot let this girl go. You have to do everything in your power to prevent her from leaving you.

145. You could live one thousand lifetimes and never impress your twelve-year-old self more.

For weeks, you continue to believe things are going well. But it's like a relationship between a toy collector and his most prized possession—keep it in the box, on display, but never to be touched or played with, definitely sitting on a pedestal. Perhaps it is more accurate to say that you hope things are going well. You do the prototypical boyfriend thing where you drive her to the airport, and actually call your mom on the ride home, admitting your official relationship to her for the first time. This public admission is a testament to the solid ground on which the relationship stands.[146] But then again, you have a notoriously untrustworthy sense of footing. Your mom contains her joy like a balloon contains air once its knot is untied. In her excitement, she explains that your little brother, a freshman in high school, also has a girlfriend now. Things are looking positively Rockwellian for her three boys.

146. See? This isn't pretentious writing at all! Just fundamentally sound linguistics.

After about two weeks of not seeing and barely talking to Dr. Valley Girl, you nail down a lunch date at In-N-Out. Along the way, you try to sneak in a few of your patented red light kisses, which are met with the tepid enthusiasm of compulsory Saturday school.

Lunch ends. You drive her back home. You feel like further conversation is a burden to her schedule and her studies. You leave without telling her how lousy you feel. The three-mile trip seems to take an hour. At least there are a few decent radio stations in Southern California. You seek through the stations for the score to your mood.

Hello there, the angel from my nightmare[147]
The shadow in the background of the morgue

Once you get home, you find the care package your mother sent for Dr. Valley Girl and binge eat the entire thing.

You really should text her how you feel. But if you do, then you'll know for sure it's over, and you'd rather just live with the possibility of a future. Don't kill Schrödinger's cat. Anyway, it would just be another interruption.

I cannot sleep, I cannot dream tonight

Is texting even appropriate? There was a huge misunderstanding in grad school last time. Would a call be … wait! Maybe this is just like that time when everything actually was okay and you're misinterpreting things!

Like indecision to call you
And hear your voice of treason.

One of the advantages of being a perpetual pessimist is never getting your hopes dashed because they're never sufficiently high. Unfortunately, you have one case of lived experience that contradicts your ordinarily rational mind. Despite all actual interpersonal evidence, your head suggests that your intuitive thinking sit this one out.

147. This will become a staple of your karaoke repertoire once you realize it's okay to have fun once in a while and forsake relentless duty to work and school. Despite lacking musical aptitude, you can kind of do the nasally voice that Tom does.

Don't waste your time on me, you're already
A voice inside my head
I miss you[xxv]

Turns out Dr. Valley Girl had felt ready to break up for weeks, but you were just too gosh darn nice for her to pull the trigger, though she had started a few times. A more appropriate taste of your own medicine could not be prescribed and dispensed.

———————

Like a squirrel who has crossed two-thirds of a busy road, you turn around to go back the way you came, erroneously perceiving it as the safer way. After six months apart, the sleepy college town of your most recent alma mater welcomes you and your packed-to-the-brim Pontiac G6 back into its arms. Plus, you can crash on your buddy's couch until you find a job.

After living a week as inverse Van Wilder, you apply for a few jobs and then take to the Appalachian Trail with one of your best friends from undergrad. He ends up doing the whole thing, and you bail after acing a phone interview in the middle of the woods of North Carolina. Two weeks and two hundred miles of magnificent hiking later, you leave the trail to return to the real world.[148] You suddenly feel more grateful for the little things, like running water and level spaces to prepare food. But these novelties wear off once you start working in the booming metropolis of Indianapolis.

During this time, your pursuit of love and romance takes a critical hit. Tinder has really taken off, and you are not exactly swipe-right material. You reason that your strengths aren't able to be appreciated in the blink of an eye, and this instant-gratification generation may very well just pass you by. Of course,

148. What an incredible experience, being plugged directly into nature during those two weeks, not worrying about anything but what was directly in front of you.

this doesn't stop you from trying and failing miserably to attract prospective partners from the app.

Three months pass, and you've proven to be as inept and unhappy with your job as you are with dating. Every morning on the drive in, you sincerely hope for a car crash on your way to work because it would be better than having to go through another day of nonsense. Your dating life feels a bit like getting T-boned as well. Your intellectual curiosity forces you to quantify just how undesirable you have become. Supposing you swipe right on twenty profiles per day, times the ninety days you have been living here, that's 1,800 potential matches. Of these, you've gotten about ten reciprocating right swipes, or about 0.006 percent when rounded.[149] This is a very unsettling feeling at a time when you could really use someplace to settle.

During this digital drought, you transition living arrangements from your twin brother's first house and your own apartment. While you are giving your money to a landlord, never to be seen again, your brother is generating equity. Living alone affords you the freedom to be an independent adult for the first time in your life and gives you the requisite privacy to have a relationship without stepping on anyone's toes, making bedroom noises too loudly, or having to compromise about whose turn it was to choose what to watch on TV.

At the conclusion of a board game night you host, most of your invitees head home, but one lingers around. Uncertain of her motivation for staying, you sit down on the couch with her and make a move, not because you are attracted to her or want a relationship but because she is physically present in the same place and time as you. This is already the most action you've gotten in months. So you land a kiss and try to go in for another.

"Would you believe this was my first kiss?"

Dear eight-pound, six-ounce, newborn infant Jesus.[xxvi]

The clouds of your depression part like the Red Sea[150] to

149. "Cowboys round up. I follow the rules of mathematics." - Dave Keammerer, 10th grade geometry teacher.

150. Allegedly.

provide you a moment of clarity: no matter how much you hurt and want or need the physical aspects of a relationship, this is not how you want that to happen. You had no idea you were stealing the first kiss from your twenty-four-year-old coworker,[151] but the thought repulses you. You apologize profusely and send her home, tail between your legs.

It is only after she leaves that a memory, long since locked away in your mental cabinetry, rushes forward. Your body had reflexively pulled away in the moment after her admission. In the same unconscious way your hand jumps back from a fire, your body had bypassed the standard cognitive process to move you to safety with expedience. Upon reflection at a later date, you remember a time where you shared her purity and innocence, only to have it taken from you without regard for your consent. Despite actively repressing the memory of the forced sexual impropriety of your youth, your brain had subconscious sense enough to pull away before you caused any more damage than you already had.

In the following months, a troubling trend rekindles your old flame, insomnia. On too many nights to count, you awaken with an insatiable longing for sex. In fact, this very sensation regularly disrupts your slumber, and it becomes normalized to the point of reflexivity, as though you are kicking off a blanket on an unseasonably warm night. Contrary to contemporary pop culture depictions of masculinity, yours is not some testosterone-fueled sexual fantasy. No, your sleeplessness is caused by the crippling desire for intimacy stemming from a complete and total bankruptcy of romantic, emotional, or intimate connection.

Necessity being the mother of invention, you try something new and experiment with an honestly communicated no-strings-attached relationship. You find a willing partner online, and for the first time, you clearly communicate your desires from the first date. It was not her preference to have a relationship based

151. Awkward alert: you would next see her on Facebook as a "Mutual Friend" a few years later with a new coworker. To cover up your shame, you ended your virtual friendship with this woman so your new coworker wouldn't ask how the two of you knew each other.

entirely around a physical connection with no emotional attach-ment, but she grows to appreciate it.

The sex is numb. It exists. It happens. But it neither excites nor delights you. It meets the minimum vascular threshold to be considered sexual intercourse rather than an exercise in rope pushing, but nothing more. You had correctly guessed that part of your depression was caused by a lack of physical and intimate connection, but you had incorrectly guessed that hooking up with someone would provide any relief. The only bright side? One time she goes on a date with another dude and bails on him mid-date to come hook up with you instead. This feels like a sexual victory,[152] and have been validated as a superior mate. So why does it feel so hollow?

152.   As though it were some contest to be won.

5

THERE IS NOTHING LEFT TO LOSE^{xxvii}

0 NEW MATCHES

Feeling like you have nowhere else to turn, you head back to the last place you felt like you enjoyed life—back to all of your friends still finishing up their graduate degrees. The week after you break the lease[153] on the room in your brother's unfinished basement, his second son is born.

This time, you have encouraged your cousin and his wife to move to town with you. The three of you, plus somewhere between two and seven cats, will live together for the next year, trying to figure out this whole life thing. You immerse yourself in

153. Figuratively, that is. What kind of monster would make you pay rent in an unfinished basement?

the process of finding a place to live, a job, and a girlfriend. For the first time in your life, your list of priorities is in this order.

Once the first two items are in order, you settle in to confront your perpetual nemesis and personal Moby Dick: the romantic relationship. Downloading, deleting, and redownloading whatever app is most in vogue has become a cycle of perpetuity and certain misfortune rivaled only by Lucy van Pelt and her football-pulling schtick.[154] Since you've returned once again to your old stomping grounds, it is a foregone conclusion that you will see some old, familiar faces in the Tinder-sphere. And you do. Ms. Transylvania, the woman you broke up with on account of tennis-related metaphors is still in town and still swiping. You instinctively panic and swipe left—but you don't forget she's in town.

After about a year and about two more failed professions,[155] you secure a real job with a real paycheck and scramble to buy a house to check *home ownership* off the proverbial checklist of successful adulthood. You invite all of the old gang[156] and your new coworkers to come warm the house, and it goes over quite well. You've inherited the Suzy Homemaker gene from your mother, and she would be so proud. One of your friends stays after all the other guests have gone. You chalk it up to her being kind and offering to help clean up, but you remain oblivious to the fact that she's flirting with you. This gets pointed out to you the next day, though, when talking to your friends en route to a hike. They've clued you in to her flirtatious ways, and you pursue a relationship.

She's nice. She's fun. Her southern accent is thick as apple butter,[157] which you find delightfully endearing. Ms. Apple Butter does extremely important work in the community for victims of rape and abuse, which you find aspirationally noble. But she smokes and has a dog (fittingly) named Smokey, so those are potential drawbacks. Overall, though, you still want to run the experiment because she's a pretty great lady.

---

154.   You own a Charlie Brown shirt, possibly for this reason, and once orchestrated an entire group Halloween costume on account of your own baldness. You regret nothing.

155.   Postal carrier and logistics coordinator. Both sucked the life out of you like Count Rugen's Machine in *The Princess Bride.*

156.   Invitations did not guarantee attendance. One of your friends missed this event and your birthday party because Ohio State was playing football. It would take you years and an unreasonable number of failed attempts to realize this was not a friendship worth preserving. Subcomment: What's the difference between Ohio Stadium and a cactus? You see, with a cactus, all of the pricks are on the *outside.*

Not all Ohio State fans are bad people, but without exception, all of the worst humans you personally know to cheer for the Suckeyes.

And things go well. She proves to be intelligent and inquisitive in addition to her more readily observable traits. The two of you find each other attractive and have no issues expressing yourselves physically. This feels healthy.

That is, until one day Ms. Apple Butter points out that you are too nice of a guy, and she wouldn't mind if you were a little rougher with her between the sheets. This feels less healthy, but you're relatively open-minded and will give it a try. After all, you aim to please. But before you can manage to ease into the rough-and-tumble slap and tickle, she has placed her forearm directly upon your windpipe, partially obstructing your airway. As you are an ardent fan of oxygen,[158] this maneuver troubles you and throws your game off, which results in her coaching, "Come on, you can do it."

Trouble is you can't. Your mental slide whistle means that there is now too much blood running to your brain to be of much service anywhere else, so the ride closes for the night. Previously, you had thought sex was a fun bonus to a relationship. This was especially true in relationships you had before losing your primary virginity because you just didn't know better. But this is a crucial learning moment for you, and for once, you don't lament the breakup. This is simply a situation where two puzzle pieces don't fit together. You certainly could have done a better job communicating the breakup with Ms. Apple Butter, but overall, it seems like a real step forward in the maturation of how you've handled relationships and breakups.

⸻

But left to your own devices, the nasty, pessimistic part of your brain starts running the show again, convincing you that you're not smart enough, not good enough, not worthy of a relationship. Having been single again for a few months, not making any

157. A list of your favorite accents, in no particular order: Australian, New Zealand, southern US, Indian. You prefer the first two for men and are comically attracted to the last two accents when spoken by women.

158. It's why you've always favored running over swimming, and when push comes to shove, the backstroke over the freestyle.

relational headway, you take out your digital rolodex, subconsciously trying to rekindle an old flame, though your conscious mind would deny it. You text Ms. Transylvania, whom you had seen on Tinder somewhat recently, to let her know that she's been on your mind and that things are going well for the first time since you were originally in grad school together.

She agrees to meet up but issues an ultimatum after you reschedule on her twice. This newfound boundary-setting, forthright version of her immediately attracts you in a way you didn't experience the first time you dated. After a few platonic meetups, she invites you to a wedding. You call her to see if she means this to be something more than friendship, and she does not. The two of you are on the same page, for once, which is encouraging. Even still, you politely decline her invitation.

But time and the blunt force trauma of solitude conspire against you both. A night together at a bourbon bar turns into you lending her your coat and then lending her floor the rest of your clothes. You have a talk about it in the morning but realize that it's okay and that you will start properly dating, unlike the last time around. This allows you to accelerate the relationship at a faster pace than if you had just met someone new; the familiarity, the shared history, and the lessons learned from previous pitfalls are already in place.

I think it's getting to the point
Where we have almost made amends

The old behaviors and habits that worked before fall back into place like matching Tetris blocks. She has a new aura about her. She seems like more of a person and less of a caricature of a graduate student. You admire her work and her seemingly new approach to having fun.[159]

And if you court this disaster
I'll point you home

159. You once told her that she was much more fun to date during your second hurrah, which she explained was a very hurtful thing to say. Somehow, you couldn't even compliment her in a way she appreciated.

Everything feels better and right this time around. You have planned a trip to Iceland in six weeks, and she seems to want to come with you. Maybe you should invite her? You've never traveled internationally before, and it would be really nice to go with someone who has.

> *You think I'm only here to witness*
> *The remains of love exhumed*
> *You think we're here to play*
> *A game of who loves more than whom*[xxviii,160]

So you invite Ms. Transylvania to join your Icelandic adventure, and she joyously agrees. You don't advertise the relationship to anyone for any particular reason, but you don't lie when a coworker asks you in a meeting if you are taking the trip with anyone. When you say your girlfriend will be joining you, six bodies turn simultaneously in their chairs and immediately start playing an unsolicited game of twenty questions with you. Your festering discomfort with answering these questions sounds off a warning buzzer in your head that you can't quite silence. Still, you go to the land of ice and snow together.

Traveling outside the United States for the first time proves to be life-changing. Henceforth, you will prioritize travel and learning about the cultures of the locales you visit. Aboard the plane in Keflavik, prior to your return to Pittsburgh,[161] you have the crystal-clear realization that this is the reason you have disposable income—to learn about, see, and experience the parts of the world labeled as unimportant or lesser than America during your formative years and adolescence.

Your relationship does not enjoy the same clarity. Your pursuit of adventure and exploration is tempered by her willingness to be timely and safe. While you are off exploring a 360-degree waterfall-turned-icicle cave,[162] she anxiously watches the clock and awaiting your return. You have exceeded the agreed-upon

160. Shoutout for grammatical correctness to the Barenaked Ladies, who are so fundamental they will be abbreviated as BNL.

161. A word to the wise—do not subscribe to Pittsburgh International Airport emails. No matter how many times you click "unsubscribe," or "report spam," their emails will hunt you down like Liam Neeson in *Taken*.

162. It's called Gljúfrabúi, and deciding to brave the slippery ice water tributary that guards it was one of the best decisions of your life. You fondly recounted the decision to your uncle who enjoyed traveling internationally, noting that you were inspired by the time he climbed over a fence in Thermopylae to visit a memorial he knew about and his tour guide didn't.

time to rendezvous, and she lets you know about it. In the moment you are being chastised for adventuring, you know it's over. From now on, you will never allow a partner to clip your wings of discovery.

You break up with Ms. Transylvania again once you get back from the trip. You renege on the commitment that it would be different this time and violate her trust. Without malice of forethought, you hurt her again, just as you had three years ago. So it goes.

—————

Much in the way gravity is constant but feels orders of magnitude greater from a cliff's edge, being single in one's thirties is exponentially more suffocating than in one's twenties. The added weight of each day without a serious partner is another quarter turn on the vice clamp around your ribcage. Avoiding this feeling makes for a compelling argument in favor of young marriage, even if time deems it to be a Type II error.[163]

You've entered the phase of your life where the space on your refrigerator once allocated for wedding invitations has given way to baby announcements. A statistically significant number of your once-wed peer group have started getting divorced, and the part of your brain responsible for panic can't help but suspect you're about to get lapped on the track of matrimony.[164]

It is occupying this headspace that you live your day-to-day life. Coupled with your long-standing anxiety and crippling self-doubt, a full-scale depression is building up momentum like an excited puppy, as best described by Patton Oswalt.[165] During your previous depressive episodes, you were unemployed, underemployed, and having existential crises about your future. This time, however, you have a job, own your house, and are

163.   Perhaps a reference to statistics doesn't really hammer this point home, but it is uniquely you.

164.   Literally within twelve hours of writing this, you got a text from a friend saying that she was engaged to be wed for the second time. The world is funny like that.

165.   See: *My Weakness Is Strong* stand-up.

recognized as a key contributor at the local and national levels for the small-ish company that employs you.

In some ways, this makes your struggles worse. Old thought patterns die hard, and you feel that your financial, professional, and platonic success ought to guarantee you a fulfilling love life because, you have been taught, good things happen to good people—ergo, you must not be a good person. But friends, family members, and coworkers keep telling you how good of a person you are …

After wearing out the gears on this cognitive merry-go-round, you realize it is easier to convince yourself that everything *is* going well and that it is relatively unimportant to be in a loving, committed relationship. You can survive without such an arrangement today, just as you always have. Or so you present outwardly.

Inwardly, however, it's a different story. The consecutive months bereft of physical contact have caused you the inability to even consider yourself a sexual prospect, let alone capable of sexual congress altogether. Folks (yourself included) often overlook this particular aspect of loneliness when they remind you that your self-worth and validation ought to be internally motivated. If this were true with respect to physical affection, you would be in good hands.[166] But it's just not true in this dimension as it is for self-worth.[167]

No, your celibacy has become a black hole whose gravity prevents even the faintest glimmer of hope from radiating out. It is in this black abyss that you take to the darkest corner of the mainstream internet—the Craigslist personals section—to try to rectify your need for physical affection.

Here, you come into contact with a world of abbreviations and euphemisms previously unbeknown to you. You flood your Google search history with queries like "FWB," "party favors," "BBW," "NSA," "water sports," and other unfamiliar terms[168] so

166. Literally.

167. Nowadays, there are businesses that try to fill this demand by providing goods and services ranging from professional cuddlers to sex dolls. Your online research for this comment necessitates a clearing of your browser history.

168. Urban Dictionary will prove to be an indispensable resource during this time.

you can try to grasp what exactly is going on in this brave new frontier of your life.

Afraid to post actual pictures of yourself, you settle for specific descriptions of your looks, your body measurements, and your intended desires. These posts are not particularly well received, and you feel even more alone than before—if not at the bottom of the barrel, are you capable of engaging in any type of relationship with anyone … ever?

Before giving up on the Craigslist experiment, you do receive a message from a couple who seem to be interested in a discreet arrangement wherein the three of you would all be engaged in a physical relationship.[169] Your immediate mental response is no. But after weighing the pain and emptiness of your recent past, you start to rationalize pursuing this sort of engagement.

At some point during this thought process, you remember that this would not be the first time you had engaged in sexual contact with another male. You recall the truth-or-dare nights in the basement without your consent. You remember your total inexperience and the degree to which your naivety was preyed upon. Had this elicit proposition come up at any point in your past, you would have politely declined on the spot. But today, you would willingly look your fourth-grade self in the eyes and explain that the pain from those experiences was not as great as the mental, emotional, and physical distress you are currently enduring. Although you have spent time every single day for the last fifteen years trying to forget how a loved one had taken physical advantage of you and your innocence, your present unmet physical and sexual needs have begun to cause you even greater hurt. Ultimately, you decline the request to become the third wheel of their tricycle and will go through a full year devoid of physical affection.[170]

169. For all the polyamorous folks - you keep on loving who you want to love in a way that works for you. This is not meant to discredit or insult your way of life.

170. It will not be the last full-year drought of intimate connection you endure.

During this incredibly dry spell, you will only periodically be able to scare up a date. As infrequent as first dates are, second dates come even more rarely. But due chiefly to sessions with a great therapist[171] and a preponderance of professional success, you begin to start deflecting personal offense to breakups, instead favoring the idea that the issue lies in how the two people fit together, not necessarily in either person. Even still, early relationship rejection stings, even if mutual fit, not personality, is the culprit.

One such rejection hits a vein of comedic gold—something far too silly to happen in real life, you would have thought. Rather, it feels like an episode ripped straight from the catalog of *How I Met Your Mother.*

You match with someone on Tinder, and you hit it off as far as small talk allows. You agree to meet up and end up sharing a perfectly nice time together over coffee.[172] The two of you share a mutual interest in travel, and she had just returned from a trip to Machu Picchu only a month or so ago. Somehow this inspires you to share your very specific, nerdy, and statistically descriptive[173] preference for air temperature. On the whole, the date seems to have gone well.

An hour or so post-date, your phone vibrates. It's a message from your coffee date, and it is a variation of the "thanks but no thanks" text to which you have never before been privy. The first line begins with the standard "you're great, but …"[174] only to take a sharp left-hand turn. Unsuspectingly, you read on: "I think you would be a really good fit for my sister."

A connoisseur of breakups and rejections alike, this is a brand-new flavor whose flowery notes have never met your lips. Your morbid curiosity has never been so succulently piqued. The

171. The two most important take-home messages from this book:
1. Mental health professionals are essential workers. Shoutout to KGM and DLG.
2. *Forgetting Sarah Marshall* is an incredible film.

172. The movie *Elf* really nails this—"coffee" and "go get food" are just code for "date." You are one of twelve people in North America who doesn't drink coffee, but explicitly explaining this before meeting someone in person would hardly place you in their good graces.

173. Assuming that room temperature is seventy-two degrees Fahrenheit, as determined by Greendale Community College, you prefer to be one standard deviation below the mean, rather than one standard deviation above. The same goes for two standard deviations. But at three standard deviations, you prefer the heat.

174. "Say no more, sir—I'll draw him from memory... You know, let me get my stencil, I think we can trace this guy and save some time." - Dave Chappelle, Just For Laughs Festival, 2007.

novelty of the proposition draws you in with the strength of a thousand electromagnets. And for her part, Big Sis is right.

Not only does Little Sis adore your microclimate preferences as described by the concept of standard deviation, but she is charmed by your way with words and attended your alma mater for her undergraduate studies as well. While you retain few fond memories of your four years on campus, there is a fondness for discussion of town lore and other shared experiences. For instance, you both agree on the best sandwich joint in town and on the best menu item they had.[175]

Your first date goes well, and you earn the right to see her again, opting to partake in a trivia challenge on a Tuesday night.[176] You select it, of course, because of its immediate proximity to the start/finish of your regularly scheduled Tuesday-night run club. She joins you straight from the gym herself and had no qualms with your relative sweatiness.

For a team of two, you do relatively well, narrowly finishing outside the money. Having enjoyed the night so far, the two of you head to the patio to talk more before calling it a night. This gives you the opportunity to ask the question that will imperil the potential for a relationship:

"Do you have any deal breakers in a relationship?"

After some careful consideration, Little Sis provides a measured response. There aren't many things that would force her to shut down a relationship, other than smoking cigarettes. After some more deliberation, she adds—or if you were an atheist.

Bullseye.

You reveal your secret identity as a nonbeliever, much to her surprise and chagrin. And would you look at that—it's suddenly crept up to her bedtime! You dutifully escort the lady to her car

175.   It's rare for a food item to live up to a cleverly hilarious name, but you'll be damned if the Tonya Harding Club didn't fit this bill.

176.   And by happenstance, you ran into a good friend of yours who would go on to help edit this very book.

before saying goodbye. She promises you can talk more thoroughly about this later, though.

True to her word,[177] Little Sis agrees to meet you for ice cream about a week later to discuss what exactly the "A word" means to you. As a card-carrying atheist, you have a pretty staunch, hardened adherence to the worldview that chaos and geographic happenstance have forced the hand of evolution for hundreds of millions of years, resulting in the cumulative effect of humanity. This is diametrically opposed to her belief in one creator who serves as judge, jury, and executioner for all living things in the cosmos. Tonight's goodbye will be your last.

Being an atheist in the Bible Belt is more than a bit precarious. Each day, you have to carefully monitor the landscape for footing with purchase and also self-censor on the fly. Every time a sneeze is met with "God bless you!" in stereo, you have to suppress the impulse to correct the concerned chorus[178] and instead play along with the social convention. You also have to refrain from twiddling your thumbs during pre-meal blessings, politely smile when people offer to pray for you[179] and assimilate to a whole host (upper- or lowercase H—both work just fine here) of other culturally accepted and unquestionable norms.

That is, unless you find someone with whom you can share your secret. The skepticism consistent with your lack of faith, however, causes you to treat each potential ally with caution, lest he or she play the O'Brien to your Winston Smith. The last thing you want is for your story to end with some light torture, brainwashing, and an expressed fealty and love of Big Brother.[180]

It is with this mindset that you continue your search for the leading lady in the production of *Your Life*,[181] your religious beliefs largely unassailed.

———

177. Perhaps the best "we need to talk" advice you could impart is this: have the talk at an ice cream parlor. If you save the relationship, great. And if not, you can tell your old pal Moose Tracks all about it.

178. The correction, of course, being that demons do not cause disease or illness. Pagans believed this and blessed whichever god was nearest by for expelling the beast by way of a sneeze. Maybe this is where the concept of Slimer was born—wait, is *Ghostbusters* an allegory for religion?

179. In the spirit of Richard Dawkins, you do enjoy offering to rebut with a hearty "And I'll think for you."

180. Er... Big Father?

181. A note to Hollywood casting agents—the male lead for this play should be Joshua Sasse. If he's unavailable, then Josh Gad. Definitely someone named Josh.

After a Tinder sabbatical of a few weeks, you return to the app like a patient to the cardiology office next to McDonald's. In relatively short order, you match with a gal from out of town whose work takes her all over the Midwest, the Midsouth, and the Mideastern states of America. You think her initial message to you sounds a bit like a bot,[182] but your inhibition has long since blown away.

You bond, again, over a mutual interest in travel and speak at great lengths about your individual experiences solo traveling to different countries. She gives you several great tips for your upcoming trip to Australia.

Deep in her eyes
I think I see the future
I realize this is my last chance

Running is of great interest to her as well, and you give her as much information on the topic as she could possibly care to know, going so far as advising her on the biomechanics of her stride. Eventually, you look at your watch, and six hours have expired. You feel as good about this as the Browns did about drafting Johnny Manziel in 2014.

She said shut up and dance with me
This woman is my destiny[183]
She said oooooh
Shut up and dance with me[xxix]

Fun little idiosyncrasies pepper your interactions with her. But in the wise words of Wanda Pierce,[184] "It's funny—when you look at someone with rose colored glasses, all the red flags just look like flags." Rather than steering clear, you downhill slalom like you're Picabo Street in Nagano.[185]

As work takes her away, fate takes her a few miles from your hometown. A short six-hour drive later, you meet up with her in

182. Bots, for the uninitiated, are fake profiles utilized for a variety of purposes. Having limited personal experience with falling for these present-day Decepticons, though, you aren't quite sure what those purposes might be.

183. At no point will you ever defend the merits of this song, but the music video is what would have happened if MGMT had directed the movie *Scott Pilgrim vs. the World*, and that's worth something.

184. You shouldn't always take advice from anthropomorphic owls in cartoon episodes about how improv, is a cult, but this time the logic checks out. Thanks, BoJack ... Horseman, obviously.

185. If you french fry when you should pizza, you're gonna have a bad time.

your original stomping grounds. Truth be told, you are visiting your grandfather in hospice care, but you make a point to sneak away from the heavy, emotionally charged family interactions to see your new lady friend. The hotel she will inhabit for the next fortnight is conveniently located right off the highway that runs between your parents' and grandparents' houses. You meet her in the lobby and feel compelled to unload the goings-on of the day, which leads to a discussion on mortality and the afterlife. After a short conversation, you are found out as an atheist.

Rather than hashing out everything right then and there, you engage in a three-hour phone call on the ride back home from your grandpa's funeral to describe the beliefs you espouse as an atheist. On the day-to-day topics, you find a tremendous overlap of beliefs about being kind to others, helping the less fortunate, and living fully.[186] But your view on the realm of the dead is just a bridge too far for her to cross.[187]

No longer will you be planning a trip to see her in Pittsburgh next month when work takes her there. To be honest, your plans for a trip to the Steel City did have an ulterior motive. One of your best friends from college is serving as a medical resident for U Pitt, and he recently got engaged to wed a Christian woman, despite his nonbelief. Maybe if the four of you could just sit in a room together and talk, you could convince your new squeeze to reconsider her foolish notion that you have to share her faith. But such a conversation never happens, and you are forced to wait for something more.

Offering to remain friends while noting that the two of you could be nothing more has become something of a forgone conclusion these days. You are starting to feel like you are putting in a lot of work, ultimately just wasting your time as much as hers—whoever *she* happens to be at the time.

186. Research on the topic will inform you that the word for this phenomenon is *orthopraxy*—the belief that doing the right deeds is the important part of a religion. You will generally agree with Christians who hang their hats on this hook.

187. Conversely, her belief system is a cross too far for you to bridge.

6

THERE'S NOTHING WRONG WITH LOVE×××

You continue to thrive at work. Despite telling you that monetary raises have been put on hold for all staff, your employer awards you three separate pay increases over the next year. You buy a house and the travel bug you caught has metastasized into a lifestyle. The president of the company knows your name and actively seeks out your expertise on a few different projects. After years of weight gain and physical inactivity, you find a magnificent running group whose members drag you out of your cave a few times a week and whip you into surprisingly good cardiovascular shape in a pretty short time. You eventually complete your first marathon, qualifying for the pilgrimage to Boston.[188] For the first time, you can sustainably afford to live by yourself, and you enjoy not having to compromise the décor motif, navigate laundry or sleeping schedules, or accommodate anyone else in any way.

But your romantic white whale is still out there as you float aimlessly aboard the Pequod. No matter how much you try convincing yourself you already have enough great things going on in your life, the emptiness from the sphere of romance starts to gnaw into other areas of your well-being, poisoning them with the same discontent. In a last-ditch effort of justifying the lack of romance in your life, you liken yourself to the aspirational Lancelot, Knight of the Round Table. While you convince yourself to be above all the worldly temptations, you more closely identify with Lance's internal turmoil as *le chevalier mal fet*, but without his adulterous rationale for self-hatred.

Despite the Arthurian drama playing out in your mind, your career as a health coach continues to fulfill your professional needs. Due to the nature of humans and of coaching, the success of each client relies heavily upon their willingness to make behavioral changes. Some folks make incredible lifestyle transformations, and their before/after pictures look like strangers. Other folks walk out the door after their first meeting, never to return. A panoply of people fall between these extremes.

Once in a while, a client comes along whom, for any number of reasons, you want to help more than others. It could be tragic life circumstances, unforgivable prejudice due to body weight, or countless other lived experiences among a list too long to recount. Before long, you realize that you have a special place in your heart for those who are about the same age as you. Perhaps it's because you were able to reverse a troubling weight-gain trend in your own life, and you are now living a wonderful, healthy life you wouldn't trade for the world.

One of the genuinely kindest, sweetest women you could

188.   Having been raised Catholic, you are no stranger to guilt, but to qualify for Boston while running only three days a week is a new level of feeling unworthy of an accolade.

ever hope to meet checks off several of the boxes above. One of the great pleasures of your week is getting to work with her. She engages with the group with a level of caring, support, and thoughtfulness you suspected was unique to saints. She buys you a Christmas present[189] out of the kindness of her heart. The day you find out she is dropping the program is not only a sad one for you, personally, but a genuine loss for the group she normally attends.

While minding your own business one day, you are introduced to a new client, whom, for some ineffable reason, you also immediately like. After some small talk chitchat, she reveals her identity as the younger sister of the saintly woman who just dropped the program. She states explicitly that her intent in joining the program is to foster a sense of well-being so that she can start a family. One of your coworkers utters the first sincere "bless your heart" in the history of the English language.

Unsure if Ms. Blessed Heart is referring to her current partner or if this is the first step in an effort to attract a special someone, a light bulb illuminates somewhere in the back of your brain.

———————

You pride yourself on maintaining your professionalism with respect to all clients, but especially Ms. Blessed Heart. In fact, you probably overcompensate and distance yourself just a little more than you would from others. Given your long history of catastrophically misjudging the intentions of others, you are never quite sure if she is just being nice or if she is actually flirting with you in a group setting. Your old pal, pessimism, guides you to the realization that kindness has been genetically selected for in her family gene pool, and there is no reason for you to get excited.

A few months pass, and you still can't make heads or tails

189.   A very punny *Lord of the Rings* shirt advertising a 5K in Mordor. You made sure to wear it when you stopped by Hobbiton during a pre-pandemic vacation New Zealand in December 2019.

of her intentions. You mention something to your boss because there have been instances at work when single male clients (and sometimes married ones) start taking a shine to their coaches. You want to make sure nothing unseemly happens and ask how the company has typically handled situations like this in the past. Your boss echoes the sentiment of your pessimism—it could be nothing, and you don't want to jump to a rash conclusion and alienate someone for whom you are providing a service.[190] The onus has been placed on the human resources department, and you are off the hook, regardless of what feelings you may or may not harbor. You have let company bureaucracy preclude you from examining your emotions any further.

Your presence is requested at the Initial Training event for new programs, where you will be presenting on how to be an effective coach to new hires. Your boss reminds you to mingle because, in spite of your aversion to small talk and pleasantries, one of your roles is to liaise the hell out of some people. In preparation for the event, you look online to see if the Los Angeles Angels of Anaheim have a home game that weekend and if there is any way you might be able to sneak out of the hotel and catch a game in your twenty-fourth different MLB stadium. Check and check.

At the beachfront hotel housing the Initial Training, the sun blazes blindingly setting over the beach view in plain sight of the patio restaurant soirée. You hob a few nobs and make sufficient small talk until you meet someone from Chicago and start asking her about her baseball allegiances, grateful for any opportunity to talk about the unexpected success of your beloved north siders. Another trainee hears this from across the patio and comes to talk trash about how much better the Cardinals are than the Cubs. You stand your ground firmly.

After a blur of networking and schmoozing, you elect to make good on an invitation from the Cardinals fan to grab a

190. This makes your boss sound like a cold, calculating woman, but you would be remiss not to clarify that she is one of the warmest, most wonderful people in your life. She was just very down to business when the situation called for it.

drink later that evening. At this point, the sun has set, and the sun no longer blinds you to her face—she is exactly the type of woman you generally never would have spoken to on account of her ravishing beauty. But here you are, so you try to play it relatively cool.

For once in your life, it works, and you have a companion for the ball game tomorrow night.

⎯⎯⎯⎯⎯⎯

The Angels are as lowly as the Cubs are inspiring this year, which means you pick up some good seats for about ten dollars apiece. When you get to the stadium, one of the ushers asks where your seats are, then suggests going down to the third base line instead because there will be plenty of unoccupied seats there (all better than the ones you bought). This serves to further the relative disbelief that any of this is actually happening to you. A nearby Angels fan covertly asks you if your female companion is a model. You don't think so but would genuinely not be surprised.

Then a nearly impossible phenomenon graces the stadium video board.

Two seconds expire in what seems like two weeks, your jaw firmly affixed to the floor. Never in one hundred lifetimes could you have imagined your face emblazoning the infamous *Kiss Cam*—least of all with the most attractive woman you have ever seen in your entire life.[191] She bails you out with a kiss on your dumbfounded, outstretched cheek.

What's left of the evening plays out with no mention of your missed kiss. You still feel like you're living in Alice's Wonderland and can't even competently order an Uber to take you back to your hotel. Things are still pretty flirty on the ride home and even on the elevator ride up. But when the door opens for the

191. Your friends back home, male and female alike, all corroborate this claim.

fifth floor, your evening comes to a close, as some of your friends would later opine, empty-handed.

Maybe because of other things in your life going so well, you choose to see this as a positive. You got kissed by a woman who was very reasonably confused for a model, and you had good conversations long after that fateful weekend. For the first time ever, you feel like you are worthy of dating someone in the upper echelon of physical appearance. By this logic, you start to believe in your own self-worth across any dimension of a relationship.

So you return home with a more positive outlook for yourself than you ever remember possessing.[192] It does not serve your dating life right away, but it is encouraging to genuinely believe good things about yourself for a change. Work and running continue to go well, and you finally take that trip to Australia you had been planning. It ends up being more magnificent than you even anticipated. Upon your return to the US of A, you go on a few dates with a girl you meet online but never really connect. Part of the problem is that when you're with her, you keep thinking about how much you'd rather be with that client from work...

192. Fueled by this feeling, you convince yourself that this is the time to start running and training again in earnest.

———

By this point, Ms. Blessed Heart has been tremendously successful in transforming her routines and thereby her physique. On one day particularly full of drear, she wears a blue pair of tights that, on more than one occasion, distracts you from the discussion at hand. Considering you are well known for discretion and your relatively unflappable demeanor, this takes some doing. You remember finding her attractive before, but this is a real watershed moment in realizing the extent to which this is true.

On blue tights night, her emotional state is inversely proportional to her appearance. You ask her if she has a minute to stick around after the group so you can check to see what is going on, and she fights back tears while telling you as little as possible. She is clearly struggling with something, but you don't feel it's your place to pry. Plus, the longer the two of you talk unsupervised, the more difficult you find it to keep your feelings to yourself. You offer a hug, subtly shifting your lower body to avoid a pelvic poke, and bid her adieu.

Months later, Ms. Blessed Heart comes into the office on a Friday, asks you a bunch of questions about your plans for the weekend, and inquires about your living situation—not in a weird way, but seemingly looking for some personal information you generally refrain from offering to clients. Your birthday is on the horizon, and she wants to know whether or not you have anything organized to celebrate. This is getting a little more personal than merits your comfort, so you go to your boss again to revisit the formal complaint that's now almost old enough to be considered a toddler.

This time, your boss asks what you think and how you feel. After you provide some dodgy answers, she needles you for an honest answer. So you tell her you have started to develop feelings for Ms. Blessed Heart and feel like the most honest thing to do would be to call and talk about it. After a confirmation from HR, you script out a rough idea of what you want to say. You send out a quick email to said client confirming a call time later that afternoon.

You watch the clock like a senior during the last class of the year, begging for the business day to end so you can hurry home to call her. Historically, your walking route home was uneventful, but on this day, you are asked to help a man in a wheelchair to traverse a bumpy sidewalk, followed by a request from a pregnant woman to help unload a washing machine from her van into her front door. It is so comical, you half expect Bugs Bunny to burrow up out of the ground, asking you for directions and lamenting his right-hand turn at Albuquerque.

With literally one minute to spare before the designated call time, you enter through the red door on the front of your house, thankful you have already produced a manuscript to begin the conversation. You call, say hello, thank her for taking a minute out of her day to chat, then launch into your prepared statement. Nervousness courses through your veins and muscles, weakening them as if you'd just run up a sand dune. Your monologue is over, and there is radio silence on the line. Eventually, she replies:

"What are you up to tonight?"

Thus begins your personal record for longest first date.

After gathering a week's supply of produce from the grocery store, Ms. Blessed Heart offers to meet you at your house, from which point you will carpool to the impressive Christmas light display on the north side of town. She feigns genuine surprise at your record collection,[193] having already stalked a picture of them from the days when you were an active Facebook user. Turns out she has put in some serious work on the ground game, trying to get to know you better without actually requesting your virtual friendship (which was strictly forbidden as per company policy).

So the two of you speed off in your Prius[194] to experience a Christmas light display, complete with an exotic animal petting zoo and hot chocolate. The two of you debate whether or not the night needs to include a camel ride and go on to say the things you never thought you'd have the chance to tell each other along the way. There are a lot of pent-up feels from the year that you have gotten to know each other.

Back at your place but in no rush to leave, she pleads to see all your vacation pictures from Australia and chides you for skipping over any. It had been past your bedtime at the start of the slideshow, and you have nearly transformed into a pumpkin at this point. How you continue to string together coherent sentences is a marvel in linguistics and the psychology of drowsiness. Ms. Blessed Heart finally has you all to herself, and she just does not want to leave. You hardly put up a fight, for your part.

There is one concern, which has stifled your enthusiasm over the past year. Her elder sister seemed like she belonged to some kind of Christian cult, which has made you concerned for the well-being of both sisters. In good conscience, you know you cannot lead on the woman sharing a seat on the couch with you. So you ask her, indirectly teasing at your fear, if she is worried

193. A surprise to literally no one still reading this.

194. Insofar as physics allows for this deliberately wacky juxtaposition.

about anything that might prevent the two of you from being happy together.

Ms. Blessed Heart correctly surmises that you do not ascribe to Christian ideologies, leading to a teary ensuing hour, but she still doesn't leave. In fact, your answer guarantees she will stay as long as possible because she believes that walking out your doorway will mark the last time she ever crosses your home's threshold. It is the final descent in the roller coaster of emotion you ride together this night.

But she still doesn't leave.

I've been waiting for this moment all my life
But it's not quite right

195. During your previous relationships, your beard was patchy and bad. You were capable of growing a rather lush moustache, but by itself, the 'stache tended to elicit the exact opposite effect.

Instead, she starts playing with your beard—something no one has ever done.[195] The sensation lives superficially on your face but also dwells somewhere deeper. This feels like a massage for your damaged ego. She is caressing away the doubt that anyone could care about you in such a way to initiate such intimate contact.

And this "real," it's impossible if possible at whose blind word
So clear but so unheard

196. An inadvertent call back to your time with the online girl in grad school. This was more of a genuine warning, though, because you weren't sure the extent to which her Christianity was conservative.

After a while, you warn Ms. Blessed Heart—if she keeps doing that, you[196] will have to kiss her. She doesn't stop, and you hold true to your word. It is a moment you had not dared to dream, but you get the sense she already had. A few minutes pass by before the silence breaks.

Everyone's so intimately rearranged
Everyone's so focused clearly with such shine

"Would you believe this was my first kiss?"
Comeon!Ohgod—thisisgettingtoberi-goddamn-diculous![xxxii]

It was one thing for this to happen when you were twenty-four, but this woman is thirty-two. You tell yourself you couldn't have known and this one isn't your fault.

Locked and loaded
Still the same ol' decent lazy eye straight through your gaze xxxi

But she still doesn't leave.

The clock strikes 3:00 a.m., then 4:00, then 5:00. It is clear that you will be getting no sleep tonight and will go straight to work without any rest. Your impromptu all-nighter comes on a Tuesday night and throws off both your sleep schedule and your workplace productivity. She regrets impacting neither. Once she leaves for work, she forgets her phone, and you chase her down. She had also forgotten her winter hat, but you only realize this after her car has carried her a quarter mile away. Her flowery scent lingers in the woolen cap.

———

Where things go from here feels a bit uncertain. It seems like there is a monolithic, immovable object preventing a long-term relationship from blossoming. But the unstoppable force of mutual affection cannot be understated. Plus, you have to give Ms. Blessed Heart her hat back, after keeping it on a nearby pillow at bedtime[197]—a token of your hopelessly romantic night together.

Arguments for and against pursuit of a relationship orbit your conversations like an electron around a nucleus. Seeming extremely far away from the origin at times, the conversation always eventually crosses back where you started. She admits to being of two minds on the entire proposition. At the end of the day, who could better understand the crushing pangs of single life in your thirties than someone who had only just had her first kiss and whose sisters were all married from within

197. A supply of zero makes for pretty high demand. A scent-bearing hat in lieu of a person makes for an odd bedfellow but coincidentally was much easier for you to fall asleep with.

their church? Her elder sister and two of her younger sisters are already married. The one who had wed outside the church has been effectively exiled from the family.

Tumultuous may be the word that which best describes the early stages of this relationship. She is wrestling with everything she has been taught to believe about love—where it can come from, who is allowed to share it, and what you are allowed to express before marriage. She has already gone against some church teachings just by locking lips with you. Many of her friends would not understand,[198] and her family would certainly disagree with her actions. The first time you meet your client at her parents' house, the matriarch reminds her not to engage in any physical contact while you are there. Because that's how the devil gets you—holding hands like a Jezebel heathen.

Tumultuous may have, on second thought, been underselling it a good deal.

Ebbs and flows are daily if not hourly occurrences. You are the lightning strike in a storm that has been brewing between her lived experience and all the orthodoxy she has been expected to internalize her whole life. When things are good, they are great. But when things are bad, they have a distinct end-times feel to them, and you never think to blame Ms. Blessed Heart. You know she is the victim of an immorally[199] narrow band of acceptable thoughts and beliefs. Such emotional torture is not of her own free will but has been the expectation of the leading men of her community. Even if the relationship fails, you hope an atheist with a big heart for humanity can help her see herself in a way not decreed as permissible by those in positions too high from which to fall.

As such, you pose a lot of questions. Some are rhetorical, and others are intended for educational purposes. You know how you feel about her in a secular sense but have to make sure there is a cognitive fit as well. For the first time in a

198. You found out that one such friend spoke of being horny but could not bring herself to even use the word. Instead, *crazy* served as a proxy. You utilized this lexicon to comedic effect at every possible opportunity.

199. You subscribe to Michael Shermer's definition of morality, which is to say that something is moral to the extent that it facilitates the thriving of all sentient beings.

relationship, you expect *her* to meet some of *your* standards. Pretty early on, you ask her stance regarding members of the LGBTQ community, and her answers scrape your threshold of acceptability like a rookie pole vaulter narrowly escaping a scratch. You have a two-page-long list of queries, which feels, ironically, like a bit of an inquisition.[200] You are, she explains, "a Christian's worst nightmare," but she suggests another family meeting to answer any questions you have, adding that her father may be better suited to answer some of your questions.[201]

He greets you with a hearty "Nice to meet you," seemingly forgetting you had spoken to him in his own house not a month ago. The first man that his second daughter had ever brought to meet the family had established no residence in his mind. You suppose it might get complicated keeping track of all eight of your children, their significant others, and their children, but it still doesn't feel great not to be remembered.

You expect many of the surface-level bits of righteous indignation—this is your daily life as an atheist observing a predominantly Christian nation. Petty handwashing bullshit like defending the forty-fifth president, claiming that King David was much worse than the reality-star-in-chief, does not surprise you. You feel like your brain needs to take a shower, but you aren't surprised. The certainty with which he waxes opinionated could strike some as believable or charismatic, but you find it accusatory and riddled with logical inconsistencies.

But you still don't leave.

And then the heavy artillery starts firing. You have lived among self-identifying Christians[202] your whole life, but never have you been subjected to a monologue from someone so inculcated into stringent teachings that he is dispensing hateful rhetoric with a smile, convinced his every word is gospel.[203]

200. Which nobody expects.

201. The thought that her father could speak to her beliefs better than she, herself, filled you with the highest level of skepticism. This seemed ugly, controlling, and like it would substantiate all of your existing biases against orthodoxy-heavy belief systems. To say that the male head of the household did nothing to change your mind was a gross understatement.

202. The lack of a clear, concrete definition garnering any serious consensus makes this the only type of Christian there is. Research and observation led you to understand that Christianity is in the eye of the beholder.

203. The central thesis of his manifesto was, to this day, the ugliest sentiment you've ever heard, and it continues to haunt you virtually every day.

Christians, he plainly states, should not be in business with non-Christians. Christians, he calmly continues, cannot engage in meaningful friendships with non-Christians. They can be acquaintances, sure, but nothing more. He concludes, using different descriptors than these, that it just isn't possible for non-Christians to add any value to the life of someone as enlightened in the ways of God as he is. Had he not already decomposed, Soren Kierkegaard would be weeping tears of joy.

You are admittedly new to reading the Bible,[204] but you are pretty sure Jesus spoke lovingly to the meek, dined with sinners, and possessed an endless acceptance of those generally labeled as enemies of Christianity. This man, your potential future father-in-law, could not more perfectly embody the opposite of such an understanding, yet he flies the flag of Christianity[205] with the confidence of someone who actually espouses viewpoints rooted in morality.

His daughter and wife sit in the den with you, wordlessly tracking his talking points. Had you not carpooled here with her, you would have walked out of his sermon long ago.

Ms. Blessed Heart assures you her father does not entirely speak for her, and they disagree that true Christians should not even be around those who don't agree with their faith, but you wonder—how much of this is baked into her worldview and will be irreconcilable? She has often claimed to be of two minds about dating you—her hive-minded upbringing in constant tension with the rational mind of a woman who has emotive and physical needs. You understand this conceptually but cannot begin to experience the turmoil with which she wrestles on a moment-to-moment basis.

After the post-sermon postmortem, you let her know she is

204. Yes, you are an atheist. Yes, you were reading from both the New and Old Testaments. Not studying these texts would be akin to skipping over the methodology section of a research paper. Plus, if you look past all the genocide and groupthink, there are some pretty good bits in there.

205. Tara Westover eloquently notices a similar holier-than-thou gatekeeping phenomenon in her family in her revelation that "the members of my family were the only true Mormons ... [and] by living with people whose faith was less, I'd become more like [the heretics]." If you haven't read her book, *Educated*, put this down and read that remarkable work instead.

welcome to stay over at your place, fully expecting her to decline. Tonight, she does as you expect,

Why are you so far away from me?
I need help, and you're way across the sea
I could never touch you—I think it wouldn't be wrong
I've got your letter, you've got my song[xxxiii]

───

After an abrupt, painful end to your relationship, you scarcely start to move on before the two of you relapse into booty call status. Ms. Blessed Heart mentions that she is going to stop reaching out to you but will be cordial to you in group sessions. After all, your profession still tasks you with coaching her, among other people. Experimenting with a complete communication hiatus arrangement, you are equal parts confused and delighted to see a text on your phone reading along the lines of:

"If you're going to dress like THAT and expect me not to tell you how great you look …"

Generally, you describe your fashion sense as "functional nonchalance," but because your sessions are being recorded and distributed to new health coaches to demonstrate the model of effective coaching, you had gotten a little spruced up.[206]

The next weekend, she comes over to your place and openly acknowledges that the two of you are not dating but, regardless, she fancies a trip around the bases with an explicit red light from the third-base coach. Dutifully, you oblige.

As the hours wane on, as has become customary at this point, she says she needs to go home despite not wanting to. Her roommates are fellow church acolytes who border on thought police. She risks serious stigma and judgment if her friends suspect you so much as hold her hand with dastardly intent. Your plea for her to stay just an hour longer revolves around a wager that

206.   You actually had to do several video shoots and wore the same shirt for the sake of visual continuity for several weeks. Corporate leadership joked that they wanted you to retire the shirt so it could be enshrined in the company Hall of Fame.

if it snows as forecasted, you can convince her it is unsafe to drive back. It does, and your gamble pays off. You have accomplished the Ted Mosby rain dance, sans cultural and ethnic reappropriation.

———

You awake the next morning, thankful for an evening of her profane mind triumphing over the sacred. The improbability of this moment transforms you into the February 3 version of Phil Connors.

The sun reflects brightly off the forecast-defying thin blanket of snow that covers the ground, and the morning glows with hope and possibility. You have curated a playlist of guilty pleasure pop songs from the nineties and early aughts, titled "Now THIS Is What I Call Music," and it fits the mood splendidly.

It's an itch we're gonna scratch
Gonna take a while for this egg to hatch
But wouldn't it be beautiful

Morning breath is an occupational hazard you would willingly pay a thousand times over for a moment like this. Having someone you love already within lips' reach as soon as you wake up? What a time to be alive.

We're at the beginning
We haven't fucked yet
But my head's spinning.

For someone who had no previous experience kissing, Ms. Blessed Heart certainly has come a long way. Chuckling to yourself, you delight in imagining the horror of her church group knowing even the tamest details of this encounter.

Why can't I breathe[207]
Whenever I think about you?[xxxiv]

At once, you are bathing in the afterglow of a wonderful evening of companionship and also ready to take on a sunny new day. Breakfast this morning will feel less like a necessary chore and more like an event you can see yourself looking forward to in the future. You'll make her an omelet to order and actually use the dining table instead of scooping mouthfuls of raisin bran down the hatch while you watch reruns of *@midnight* from the living room couch. You'll start spinning Alabama Shakes' first record while washing the dishes, and it will be an excellent start to a day full of possibility.

And it pretty much goes like this.[208] With respect to unbridled contentment, this morning reminds you of the night around Christmas when you had bought her a Rudolph-themed onesie and watched *A Muppet Christmas Carol* together. Watching her jump up and down on the bed that yuletide night with the carelessness of a child, you really felt like kindred spirits destined to be together.

This afternoon, however, is not such a good afternoon.

Ms. Blessed Heart's roommates were highly suspicious when she had not made it back home last night, and the devil did some of his finest work at night, they scolded. You can't possibly know the extent to which she has been made to feel guilty, but you assume the versions of the stories she relayed to you were merely iceberg tips. This being the case, you cannot imagine how difficult this must all be for her—faith and her first love, embattled in a ceaseless tug-of-war. Your beliefs afford you the luxury of just caring about her without regard for what anyone else thinks of your behaviors. Such is the invisibility of privilege.

She needs to go completely off the grid for a bit to think and pray on what to do next. While you do not see the benefit of such practices yourself, you are very supportive of her engaging with her God to determine the best path forward. Your cynicism

207.   Say what you want about Liz Phair, but for a pop song, this fucking bops. That's why it leads off this playlist.

208.   Independently of what the future holds, you will always remember this morning with a particular fondness for the sheer joy it brought you in the moment.

has prevented you from being surprised when each of her divine powwows up to this point has included you in her plans. Confirmation bias, you know, holds at least as much strength in the mammalian brain as religion and ritual.

You don't know the exact precipitating factor in the subsequent radio silence,[209] but it is related to the pious team yanking the carnal team's end of the rope sufficiently far enough to cause a pileup. Surprisingly enough, this surprises you.

By this time, you had expected the relationship was home free—the first breakup was the tough one, and every subsequent time Ms. Blessed Heart picked you over orthodoxy, she would be more and more likely to do it again. You had even professed, after the first relapse, that you loved her but could not continue the on-again, off-again dating. She was either in or out, and for the first time, you realize she really is out.

You had suspended your unflinching atheism with respect to Christianity, instead favoring an approach of "What can I learn from this ideology?" In fact, the first time she told you that you couldn't be together on account of your faithlessness, you quoted George Bailey, asking her to "Show me the way." You have been battered around enough by the single life and are willing to overturn every rock of what you think you know if it means leaving solitude behind for a while.

Truth[210] be told, you want to believe in her God. Believing that good things are going to happen to good, godly people sounds like a brilliant solution. You could forsake your anxiety for trust in a divine plan. You could be emboldened by the fact that an afterlife exists, and you could rejoice when eventually reunited with your lost loved ones. You would be imbued with the ability to seek all the beauty of life in[211] every animated object.

209. You would call it a breakup, but she would not, because she did not consider the two of you to be dating at the time. Insistent deduction (rather than induction) has a knack for turning the least flexible among us into gold-medal mental gymnasts.

210. Capitalized because it's the start of a sentence, not as a vote of confidence for Christian orthodoxy.

211. Ah, the crux of the issue. There is more than one way to seek beauty—no one ideology has a monopoly over the lovely and beautiful!

Christianity could promise an eternal lazy river sans sunburn with this wonderful woman in an adjacent inner tube—if only you could be moved to believe in it.

So you tried. You had conversations with your sister-in-law, who had been praying for your salvation for years.[212] She recommended a book, Brian Zahnd's *Sinners in the Hands of a Loving God*.[213] You read Kierkegaard,[214] bought a book advertised on Christian radio called *Inexpressible: Hesed and the Mystery of God's Lovingkindness*, and scoured the internet for any video or resource you could possibly find to convince you the divine providence of a desert handyman.

It just doesn't exist.[215]

At least not in a way that is compatible with maintaining a relationship with Ms. Blessed Heart. And despite the tremendous self-growth that has stemmed from your research, you still feel a little hollow. The person for whom you have longed—the tangible, touchable, kissable person who has listened to garbage nineties songs with you, the person who has jumped around like a jubilant child on your bed—can never be the person you will grow old with. This reality hurts more than seems reasonable.

Knowing the potential for a relationship is now over, you speak very candidly about how much you still care about her as a person. You let her know that you have no regrets regarding the relationship, and you are especially glad that so many items in her list of physical-affection firsts were crossed off with the pen of love rather than of power or lust. She appreciates this more than you may ever know, and she understands why it is so important to you. When you tell her about your sexual abuse, she claims to have known something traumatic had happened to you. She says it was hard to qualify or quantify exactly, but even before you had started dating, she sensed you were carrying a great pain.

Having been an unwilling passenger during your first journey into sexual contact, you are particularly heartened that Ms. Blessed

212. This sounds nice, it really does. But no matter what you believe, if you pray for someone to think exactly like you do, then you are condemning them to groupthink, which is a group text invitation to the gates of hell.

213. A wonderful read, by the way!

214. A judgmental, hate-filled read, by the way!

215. One of your friends started referring to the novel coronavirus epidemic as the zombie apocalypse in late March. You admitted to him and yourself that if a horde of undead beings emerged on Easter in 2020, Christianity would finally meet your burden of proof, and you would get baptized on the spot, as antithetical as that would be to the whole concept of faith.

Heart's narrative does not have to include the same dark backstory. You explain that being able to provide her a healthier sexual alternative to your past is worth more to you than Bill Gates' fortune.[216]

216.   Words by which you still stand to this day.

———————

Ghosts of relationships past will always haunt you if you let them. Your perceived failures to secure a stable, long-term relationship have motivated you to determine that this relationship will be your last, out of fear that another would end like all the rest. Since day one, you had treated this relationship as though it would lead to marriage rather than taking an honest appraisal of the context and seeing it as a nice house built on a really rocky foundation. Again, your rose-tinted eyes found red flags to be imperceptibly different from green ones.

So in this moment, you wonder why everyone you like or love continues to reject you. You wonder, particularly in the case of the three most recent Christian women—how could they see your actions, your behaviors, how you treat other people, and decide that you aren't good enough? Why couldn't they be with you just because you have a different name for what you experience when a moment exudes spirituality? The more you research, the more you understand what Christianity means to you—and your definition compels you to love unabashedly and without restriction based on ideological differences.

But such revelatory hindsight is only gained by a year or so of space and reflection. In the moment, you are made to feel less than and unworthy of love for not being pious enough. This realization pains you in a way that no other human could make you hurt. Your heart breaks for those who are ruled by such an exclusive, lonely worldview.

You suppose there is very little left for you in your current milieu, so you quit your job and move across the country.[217]

217.   You would secure a job and a place to live before actually moving, though. Romanticism often shares a border with lunacy, but this was no such case.

See also, Raphael Bob-Waksberg's short story by the same name - *Move Across the Country*.

7

BENEATH THE SKIN^{xxxv}

A decade has passed since one of your relationships lasted more than two months.

In this time, you've witnessed the online dating game endure a few paradigm shifts. First, there were the free websites with simple names, like Match and eHarmony. But as is inevitable in the West, capitalism took root and monetized these sites in the service of shareholder-pleasing ventures. Eventually, these sites reduced their free trial periods from a month to a week to nothing at all.[218] Others, like Zoosk, claimed to be free but charged by desired functionality. You could create a profile without charge, but you couldn't send messages without paying. Then came the Craigslist of dating—Plenty of Fish. Last you

218. TANSTAAFL—There Ain't No Such Thing as a Free Lover.

219. At one point, you discovered that you and your brother, eleven years your junior, were both using the site at the same time and in the same city. Indianapolis is by no means a small city, but the thought that someone equidistant in age from you could have gone on a date with each of you... Inconceivable!

220. Barry Bonds and Willie Mays pose the most obvious cases. Ty Cobb and Ted Williams from a universe without World War II can also stake a serious claim. Back to the story before you start analyzing fWAR versus bWAR...

221. After deliberation, you decided against using the "whored" in this text so as to not sully the name and reputation of sex workers.

When you've spent dozens of pages making jokes and sarcastic quips, you paint yourself into a corner, but the above comment is wholly sincere.

222. "MSSR" to the savvy dating SABR-metrician.

used it, everything was completely free, but there were more bots and riffraff than suitable mates. You ended up having halfway decent success on OKCupid,[219] which attempted to turn love into a math equation, appealing to all the logical parts of your brain. It led to several promising dates (including several of the aforementioned). But ultimately, you succumb to the behemoth of Tinder.

Given the advent of phone applications, GPS functionality, and the convenience of pocket-sized technology, the ubiquity of cell phones was a foregone conclusion. This perfect storm turned Tinder into the Babe Ruth of dating: arguably not the best[220] but unquestionably synonymous with the game.

You recently relocated to the West Coast again for a multitude of reasons. Feeling as though you have fished out your nearest pond in the Bible Belt, you are excited by the prospect of re-downloading Tinder in your new home state. But then again, Charlie Brown had thought the same thing about kicking field goals.

Nowadays, Tinder is not used exclusively for securing hookups and dates. Bots run rampant, social media influencers sell themselves[221] to harvest social media followers, and your mutual swipe-right rate[222] makes the Mendoza Line blush. As such, the likelihood of even clicking through a profile to learn about someone is an all-but-forgotten practice. But then one profile stops you cold in your tracks, and you become enraptured with the splendor that is Christina.

Her smile grabs you, straight out of the gate. Her linked music profiles pluck at your hipster heartstrings. Her hot-chocolate-brown eyes would melt you like a marshmallow if ever they got the chance. You don't even swipe right for a while; if she doesn't reciprocate, this moment will have fleeted. Sufficiently wowed, you do your best to capture photographic memories before taking the plunge into the abyss and uncertainty of swiping right.

Geographic happenstance is not your only luck this evening—she has already liked your profile! You are afforded the luxury of replacing the anxious waiting for affirmation with the anxiety of determining the appropriate amount of time to wait before sending a message. Your immediate reaction is a combination of relief and joy that she even likes you. That is, until you remember the bit about the bots and those trying to buy IG influence. But for a moment, you are rather pleased with yourself.

An appropriate amount of time later, you message her, get a response, and set up a date before the week's end. After getting lost on your way to the agreed-upon coffee[223] spot, you walk in through the front door. Christina is speaking to the barista like they are old friends, her kindness effervescent. This woman has already exceeded your lofty expectations, and suddenly you're glad you bailed last night on the girl you had met at the karaoke bar last weekend.

Christina is engaging, funny, fun, inquisitive. She gives off an aura of authenticity. Alanis Morissette once sang of the desire for "intellectual intercourse," and it is clear your Tinder match could easily satisfy this desire. After a post-beverage walk but before parting ways, the truth spills right out of you.

You tell her that she's a lovely person and that you'd really like to see her again.

———

Upon your return from a spontaneous trip to New Zealand, you set up a second date with Christina. Considering that Christmas has just passed, you agree to dinner and a stroll down a street notorious for its over-the-top, communal holiday décor.[224] Next on the docket is ice cream, and she knows just the place. As

223. Coffee, again, in the colloquial sense, as humorously noted in the movie *Elf*.

224. You don't just call your neighborhood Candy Cane Lane—it's a title bestowed upon you.

you stroll through the neighborhood, you learn a good deal about Christina, and you are on board with an eerie amount of what she says. She wants to live in a tiny house? Her firstborn is named after a Tolkien character? She is looking for a serious relationship? She wants to help others combat systemic racism in health care? She wants to read your published research about gender disparities in print magazines? Putty, meet hand.

Days and dates continue to go exceedingly well. So well, in fact, that you even mention your recent string of promising dates during the morning meeting at work, in front of about thirty coworkers, most of whom are still relative strangers. Your office has rooftop access, and you have half a mind to use it as your personal megaphone. Responsibly, you resist the urge—at least for today.

Karaoke,[225] intellectual conversations, daily texting, and other proxies for a successful relationship all seem to be moving in the right direction. Not to mention, her forthright and transparent honesty are a dream come true. You are emboldened to invite her to a party with your coworkers[226] the following week. She accepts the invitation.

At the end of a lovely evening of board games and socializing, your only concern is that she has to leave so early the next morning to orchestrate childcare, but such is the life of a single mother. It feels to you as though the relationship is months old, when in fact you haven't even reached your month-iversary just yet. You start warming up to the idea that perhaps the solitude of your personal Groundhog Day is approaching its inevitable conclusion.

The breakneck pace of your digital communication inevitably slows, chagrined though you are. She's working full-time, taking graduate-level courses, and coparenting two kiddos.[227] You're genuinely glad she's got any time for you at all. In another display of sincere emotion, you thank her for making time

225. You had the courage to debut your rendition of Violent Femmes' *Blister in the Sun* when out with Christina. It went surprisingly well!

226. She had mentioned a previous bad experience with dating someone but never really seeing them in social settings, so you may have fast-tracked this just a little bit to see if you passed her criteria for an acceptable mate.

227. Badass alert!

to hang out and admit that you are startled by how much you like her. Christina's continued openness, honesty, intelligence, and homemade green chile sauce have only exacerbated these feelings. But you start to wonder: is this word vomit of emotion causing her to pull away?

———

Before long, dating Christina turns into a slow-moving panic attack. Supply of her attention has bottomed out, while your demand has concurrently peaked. What little chill you ordinarily possess has long since depleted.

If being lovestruck were rated like skin burns, you would have it in the third degree. It's gotten so bad that you can't even keep your phone within arms' reach, lest you obsessively[228] check. Into the breakroom your phone goes, relegated to three daily checks during anxiety-riddled breaks in the morning and afternoon, plus lunch.

Whenever you are treated to a text response, bliss befalls you, and relief washes over you like the tide. Initially anyway. Eventually, you begin to study and mull over her messages with your trademark scholarly precision, hoping to synthesize backstory, context, and inside jokes to formulate the perfect reply. What actually results is a series of bloated, bulky texts reeking of desperation. You get the sense you're about to get snuffed out.

True, openness and honesty characterize this relationship, but you have not yet had the exclusivity conversation. One of your coworkers is trying to set you up with a friend, and you want to get ahead of potential trouble. You're obviously crazy about Christina, but explicitly broaching the topic of dating or not dating other people seems like a good idea. If you can just get a hold of her over the phone, this is exactly what you intend to do. In your head, this conversation will serve as an affirmation

228.   A healthy phone/life balance has long since eluded the American public, but you have tended to manage it well. Now, however, you are at the whim of technology, and it's not a good look for you.

229. Like summoning Biggie Smalls or Beetlejuice, using the phrase "in your head" one more time will conjure a spectral Dolores O'Riordan to belt a few bars of The Cranberries' *Zombie*.

230. It is explained to you later that your message daftly misses these ideals.

of your commitment and show that you're serious enough about her to flat-out refuse a date with someone else. But the only place this conversation happens is in your head.[229]

When you send the "let's talk" text, she lets you know she won't be available for the next couple of days to set up a time to talk with you. Your chest implodes. You notice that the hallmark psychosomatic distress, which has become synonymous with these situations, has returned. You want to cry, puke, leave work, and jump out of the fifth-story window—and not necessarily in this order. Order is given no quarter in your present mental state. Instead, you craft a text response forthright in nature. The message aims not to be accusatory or unkind in nature,[230] but to let her know that this relationship is no longer working for you. All that's left to do now is wait for a reply, which you realize may never come.

During a designated phone check-in on your afternoon break, you see Christina has responded, noting how good it is to be on the same page because she had also intended to end things. She also reveals that on the night of your coworker get-together, she was magnetically attracted to one of your colleagues and was getting major reciprocated vibes. Before you have the opportunity to ask her not to reveal the identity of this crush, she lays it bare.

Pop quiz: why does this feel like an unnecessary sting to you? Is it:

A. You frequently complimented Christina's looks out of sheer admiration and sincerity.
B. In your time together, you initiated all physical contact past first base.
C. You interact with this coworker on a daily basis, and your rampant insecurities reflexively cause you to compare yourself to them during each interaction. Given this

evidence, you are forced to concede your relative unattractiveness by this, the only metric of consequence.

D. Here we go again. This happens every time, and you feel doomed to this somewhat superficial fate for the umpteenth time.

E. All of the above.

Of course, you know the answer is E and award yourself one hundred points for responding correctly. Collect enough arbitrary points, and you could buy yourself one of those cool snap bracelets from middle school or something. This train of thought was lifted directly from a conversation you had with Christina, wherein she awarded you a thousand points on a few separate occasions for taking care of the cooking duties. The playful memory hearkens back to a time when things were fun and easy, filled with silly banter. It's exactly this type of inside joke and intimate knowledge that you will miss moving forward. And then…

All of these memories come rushing
Like feral waves to your mind

At once, the results of every past romantic autopsy well up in your throat. You watch an instant replay of all the inside jokes from your relationships emeritus: pitchers and catchers reporting for duty. Peeing like a racehorse. The Sex Dungeon. Boo-Boo. Niecelings.

Of the curl of your bodies
Like two perfect circles entwined

The phenomenon spreads to the mistakes you've made and the painful lessons learned from previous relationships. A stolen first kiss. Smash and roll clementines to remove the peel in one fell swoop.

And you feel hopeless and homeless

It can snow at temperatures below thirty-two degrees. Obsessive compulsive disorder is a real thing. Two parts peanut butter to one part jelly makes the ideal sandwich.

The world is falling 'round you

The door by the backup gym at the middle school can be yanked open, and you can make out in the back hallway. Chalk-stencil prom proposals. Sock hops on the middle school basketball court.

You just have to see her

Another stolen first kiss. Infidelity. Talks with HR. Pillow fights after high school dances.

All these memories coalesce into a phantasmic amalgam of unrequited love and heartbreak—an anthropomorphic specter of your past. The line between breakup and baby panic attack continues to blur beyond recognition.

And you know that she'll break you in two[xxxvi]

Unsure if her mutual desire to end the relationship makes things better or worse, you simply try to put it out of your mind. From experience, you know this will help you lead your daily life, pay your bills, sleep better at night, and repeat it all again. That is, until you get a message a few days later reminding you of your outstanding lent copy of George Orwell's *1984*. The origin of the message is from the last person of whom you want to be thinking, and you certainly do not want to be in conversation with her. In equal measure of nihilism and generosity, you offer the book to Christina and end the saga.

———————

Or so you thought.

Thanks to a meltdown-inspired text[231] that would have greatly benefitted from a table of contents, the two of you are getting pizza together on a Friday afternoon to talk about how the contents of your deliberately crafted but unfortunately worded breakup text

231. In a plot twist, she has the meltdown, not you. Who would've guessed?

made Christina feel terrible. Other topics, of course, are also on the table—all of which would have better served the relationship had they been said a week or two prior. But here you are, fortuitously late rather than not at all.

Tucked into your front pocket is the list of topics you want to address, most of which are apologies for having become a jealous, crazy person rather than a supportive partner. Christina accepts your apology, despite not necessarily noticing your transformations to and from Jekyll and Hyde. She is also relieved beyond measure that your breakup text was not intended to be malicious or mean-spirited. Smiles creep to the corners of both your faces.

So you continue making your way down the list stashed in that breast pocket of yours. You speak, listen, discuss, and reconcile each bullet point. This begins to feel like the healthiest, most mature adult relationship you have ever experienced.

Lunch ends with a mutually warm, wholehearted embrace. And you both live happily until the end of your days.

Albeit, not together.

EPILOGUE
IS THIS IT^{xxxvii}

Six thousand six hundred fifty-two words,[232] spread across twelve lengthy emails, turn your brain into a concrete mixer. The fact that all this communication happens amid a global pandemic tugs at your single-fiber tether to reality. These digital soliloquies come from a source you would have deemed unlikely until about a week ago. Another former weight-loss client of yours has reached out to explain in explicit detail how she felt and continues to feel about you. The conclusion to M. Night Shyamalan's *Sixth Sense* surprised you less than these revelations.

232. Not quite as catchy as that little number from *Rent*...

Your immediate thought is a selfish one: what if this is the only way you are capable of attracting women? What if they only like[233] you because of the role you've played in helping them lose weight? What happens when you like someone who doesn't want or need to lose weight? What chance do you have at a serious long-term relationship if your only gambit is useless?

How have you become a one-trick pony? … Wasn't this the name of the book Diane Nguyen wrote about BoJack Horseman? Oh god, have you become BoJack? But since you wrote the book, does that mean you're Diane? Are you the bastard lovechild of Diane and BoJack, replete with all their insecurities and none of their strengths?

Has all of your experience been in vain? Can any of the romantic hardships you've endured propel you forward in a positive way? Even if most of those hardships were, in retrospect, self-imposed?

Prisoner on the loose

Why is your pulse racing? Is it getting harder to breathe? How long would it take someone to find you if you collapsed right now?

Description: a spitting image of me

Do you have enough PTO to just go home, or do you have to pull your shit together and stay at work? Having been a manager before, you would feel guilty getting paid for panicking rather than working …

Except for a heart-shaped hole where the hope runs out

You work in health care—why do you even have to use PTO for what should be considered a sick day? Should you fill out a PHQ-9 and a GAD-7? Would this quantifiably validate your mental state, even though the straw that broke your back (or in this case, your sanity) was some woman emailing you about how much she likes you?

With my toes on the edge, it's such a lovely view

What if you already missed your best shot at happiness? Who was the one that got away? Have you already met the woman you are "destined" to marry, or is she still out there?

I never loved anything until I loved you

How much time is left on your break? What if people are looking for you to get back to work? What if someone notices you right now, in this state?

I haven't a thing unless I have you.

What if no one notices? What if you are so expendable that your absence isn't even noticed? Which would be worse? What if you add no value to this company *or* to the lives of the women you date?

I'm over the edge, what can I do?

If you define yourself by work and relationships, and you are failing both, what are you doing with your life? How are you so bad at it? Why have you wasted your time doing what you were taught was the right thing when it all leads to this? What is the goddamned point of it?

I've fallen through[xxxviii]

That baby panic attack you started having when your last relationship ended? It's all grown up.

———

You have been a medical assistant at a family care practice in Seattle in the midst of the novel coronavirus pandemic, and COVID-19 is presently your second biggest worry. Understandably, everyone is experiencing some existential worry, and perhaps it is this fear of historical and present loneliness in times of such uncertainty which escalate your sense of dread pertaining to romance. You feel like you've wasted your entire life by never satisfying the pop culture-fueled ambition of getting married, and life could be ending any day now. A single thread tethers you to reality, preventing you from losing your mind, and its elasticity is being stress tested with every outbreak update and every recollection of your failed dating history.

You are now eight weeks deep into your Zoloft-laden life, and apart from your extraordinarily loose stools,[234] things are actually better than they had been. Aided by reflection, the passage of time, and the wisdom of your therapist, you are able to talk yourself down from the mental ledge, much to the chagrin of your old pals anxiety, depression, melancholy, sadness,[235] self-doubt, and panic.

You start to wonder, now that the mental fog has subsided, what if the women who have most recently admitted their feelings did so because you honestly expressed yourself to them as a coach?

So I take off my face
'cause it reminds me how it all went wrong

What if those feelings were genuine because you were being genuine to them? What if, for the first time, these were examples of you demonstrating your vulnerability to folks, and they were responding in truthful kind?

And I pull out my tongue
'cause it reminds me how it all went wrong

What if these women have all seen kindness, compassion, and sincerity because you actually possess those traits and have been given a professional platform in which you can showcase a high-fidelity version of your genuine self?

234. Your late maternal grandfather often described these symptoms as being able to "poop through a straw." Remembering his witticism usually makes you crack a smile, even when symptomatically perched on your porcelain throne.

235. Finite sadness, admittedly.

And I cough up my lungs
'cause they remind me how it all went wrong

You start to believe that this logic has some traction, instead of confirming your worst fears about your biggest shortcomings and a belief that no one could have such deep positive feelings about you. Maybe this was just an expression of pure human connection with women who were deprived of compassion in the same ways you have felt. Maybe extending decency, courtesy, and understanding to one another isn't the norm these days, and this combination of traits is exactly what makes you desirable in their eyes. Maybe love is meant to be shared indiscriminately among friends, family, coworkers, and strangers—not with the explicit intent of securing romantic stability but because the process of doing so makes everyone feel seen, respected, and human. Maybe the reward is the rainbow and not the pot of gold put on a pedestal by every aspect of Western society.

But I leave in my heart
'cause I don't want to stay in the dark[xxxix]

You suppose that maybe, just maybe, all of this is the case.

ENDNOTES

i   *Cracked Rear View*. Hootie & the Blowfish. Atlantic Records, 1994. Produced by Don Gehman.

ii   *Bad Self-Portraits*. Lake Street Dive. Signature Sounds, 2014. Produced by Sam Kassirer.

iii   "Motion Sickness," 2017. Written by Phoebe Bridgers and Marshall Vore. Produced by Tony Berg and Ethan Gruska.

iv   "Amazed," 1999. Written by Marv Green, Chris Lindsey, and Aimee Mayo. Produced by Dann Huff and performed by Lonestar.

v   *"Everything You Want,"* 2000. Written by Matthew Scannell. Produced by Mark Endert and Ben Grosse, and performed by Vertical Horizon.

vi   *Era Vulgaris*. Queens of the Stone Age. Interscope Rekords, 2007. Produced by the Fififf Teeners.

vii   "Self Esteem," 1994. Written by Dexter Holland. Produced by Thom Wilson and performed by the Offspring.

viii   "Too Close," 1997. Written by Kay Gee, Terry Brown, Robert Huggar, and Raphael Brown. Produced by Kay Gee and performed by Next.

ix   "I Love You Always Forever," 1996. Written by Donna Lewis. Produced by Donna Lewis and Kevin Killen and performed by Donna Lewis.

x   "What's a Guy Gotta Do," 2004. Written by Don Sampson, Joe Nichols, and Kelley Lovelace. Produced by Brent Rowan and performed by Joe Nichols.

xi   "The Sound of Settling," 2003. Written by Ben Gibbard. Produced by Chris Walla and performed by Death Cab for Cutie.

xii   "Up in Arms," 1997. Written by Dave Grohl, Nate Mendel, and Pat Smear. Produced by Gil Norton and performed by Foo Fighters.

xiii   "Down in a Hole," 1992. Written by Jerry Cantrell. Produced by Alice in Chains and Dave Jerden. Performed by Alice in Chains.

xiv   *We Were Dead Before the Ship Even Sank*. Modest Mouse. *Epic*. Produced by Dennis Herring.

xv   Vealey, *Coaching for the Inner Edge*, 1st edition (Morgantown, WV: Fitness Information Technology, 2005).

xvi   "Still the One," 1997. Written by Robert John "Mutt" Lange and Shania Twain. Produced by "Mutt" Lange. Performed by Lake Street Dive.

xvii   "Let Her Cry," 1994. Written by Mark Bryan, Dean Felber, Darius Rucker, and Jim Sonefeld. Produced by Don Gehman and performed by Hootie and the Blowfish.

xviii   "Wake Me Up Before You Go-Go," 1984. Written, produced, and performed by George Michael.

xix   "Falling for You," 1996. Written by Rivers Cuomo. Produced and Performed by Weezer.

xx   "Tell me I'm Pretty," 2015. Cage the Elephant. RCA. Produced by Dan Auerbach.

xxi   "Time Warp," 1973. Written by Richard O'Brien and Richard Hartley. Performed by Riff Raff, Magenta, the Criminologist, Columbia, and Transylvanians.

xxii   "Kiss the Girl," 1989. Written and produced by Alan Menken and Howard. Performed by Samuel E. Wright.

xxiii   *The Princess Bride,* 1987. Written by William Goldman. Produced by Andrew Scheinman and Rob Reiner. Distributed by Twentieth-Century Fox.

xxiv   Lynne Truss, *Eats, Shoots & Leaves* (Profile Books, 2003), 228 pages.

xxv   "I Miss You," 2003. Written by Tom DeLonge, Mark Hoppus, and Travis Barker. Produced by Jerry Finn. Performed by blink-182.

xxvi   "Talladega Nights," 2006. Written by Adam McKay and Will Ferrell. Produced by Columbia Pictures, Relativity Media, and Apatow Productions.

xxvii   "There Is Nothing Left to Lose," 1999. Foo Fighters. Roswell/RCA. Produced by Foo Fighters and Adam Kasper.

xxviii Call and Answer," 1998. Written by Steven Page and Stephen Duffy. Produced by Barenaked Ladies, David Leonard, and Susan Rogers. Performed by Barenaked Ladies.

xxix   "Shut Up and Dance," 2014. Written by Ben Berger, Eli Maiman, Ryan McMahon, Nicholas Petricca, Kevin Ray, and Sean Waugman. Produced by Tim Pagnotta. Performed by Walk the Moon.

xxx   "There's Nothing Wrong with Love," 1994. Built to Spill. *Up*. Produced by Phil Ek.

xxxi   "Lazy Eye," 2007. Written by Brian Aubert, Christopher Guanlao, Joe Lester, and Nikki Monninger. Produced by Dave Cooley. Performed by Silversun Pickups.

xxxii   "Anchorman," 2004. Written by Adam McKay and Will Ferrell. Produced by Dreamworks, Apatow Productions, and Herzon-Cowen Entertainment.

xxxiii   "Across the Sea," 1996. Written by Rivers Cuomo. Produced by Weezer on Geffen Records. Performed by Weezer.

xxxiv   "Why Can't I?" 2003. Written by Lauren Christy, Graham Edwards, Liz Phair, and Scott Spock. Produced by the Matrix on Capitol Records. Performed by Liz Phair.

xxxv   "Beneath the Skin," 2015. Of Monsters and Men. *Republic*. Produced by Of Monsters and Men and Rich Costey.

xxxvi   "Sometime Around Midnight," 2009. Written by Mikel Jollett. Produced by Pete Min on Majordomo Records. Performed by The Airborne Toxic Event.

xxxvii   "Is This It," 2001. The Strokes. RCA/Rough Trade. Produced by Gordon Raphael.

xxxviii "I Appear Missing," 2013. Written by Joshua Homme. Produced by Dean Fertita, Joshua Homme, James Lavelle, Michael Shuman, and Troy Van Leeuwen on Matador Records. Performed by Queens of the Stone Age.

xxxix   "Organs," 2014. Written by Nanna Bryndís Hilmarsdóttir, Ragnar Þórhallsson. Produced by Rich Costey on Republic Records. Performed by Of Monsters and Men.

Printed in the United States
by Baker & Taylor Publisher Services